世遗之城：泉州

QUANZHOU: A WORLD HERITAGE CITY

美美与共——宋元泉州的多元社群

Beauty Represents Itself with Diversity and Integrity: Diverse Communities in Song-Yuan Quanzhou

中共泉州市委宣传部　编

海峡出版发行集团 | 福建人民出版社
THE STRAITS PUBLISHING & DISTRIBUTING GROUP | FUJIAN PEOPLE'S PUBLISHING HOUSE

目 录

Contents

引　言

泉州，一座写满海洋记忆的港口城市。她以包容友善的心态接纳着不同肤色、语言和宗教的外来族群，共同塑造了这座城市生动多彩、充满活力的社会风情和文化多样性城市景观，堪称世界历史进程中东西方文明交流互鉴的杰出代表。

宋元时期，海洋贸易的不断发展，不仅为泉州带来了巨额的财富，也使泉州成为令人向往的国际大都市。数以万计来自亚洲、非洲、欧洲的商人与传教士聚居在这个流光溢彩的港城里，与此地的皇族、官员、士族及平民一起构成宋元泉州的多元社会群体。他们不仅在泉州经商、传教和生活，还参与到泉州本地的诸多社会事务中，甚至与当地汉人通婚，世代居留。他们有的成为巨商，有的当上高官，成为一方权贵。不同身份、文化背景的群体在这里相遇相处，使宋元时期的泉州社会成为不同文化的汇聚中心，成为一座世界性的东方城市；同时使泉州成为极富世界性交往维度的商业型社会，这不仅推动泉州整体繁荣并跻身世界贸易港口中心，也在泉州留下独特而光辉灿烂的多元文化史迹。

泉州，这座被刺桐花掩映的美丽海港城市，以Zaitun或Zayton（即“刺桐”）之名蜚声海外。当你漫步古城的街巷时，三步一庙，五步一堂，各种宗教、不同民族跨越时空在这里相遇并和谐共处，为世界保留下“大航海时代”之前人类航海及贸易活动的历史记忆。

泉州古城。（陈英杰 摄）
The ancient city of Quanzhou. (Photo by Chen Yingjie)

Introduction

Quanzhou, a port city filled with memories of the sea, embraces immigrant communities of different skin colors, languages, and religions with a mindset of inclusiveness and kindness, thus shaping the vibrant, dynamic social customs and cultural diversity of the city. It is an outstanding representative of the exchange and mutual learning between Eastern and Western civilizations in the world history.

During the Song and Yuan Dynasties, the continuous development of maritime trade not only brought huge wealth to Quanzhou, but also made the city an internationally attractive metropolis. Tens of thousands of merchants and missionaries from Asia, Africa, and Europe settled in this glittering port city. Together with the local imperial family, officials, literati, and commoners, they constituted Quanzhou's pluralistic social groups in the Song and Yuan Dynasties. They engaged in business, preach and daily life in Quanzhou and participated in local social affairs, even intermarried with local Han people and resided for generations. Some of them turned into wealthy merchants, while others high-ranking officials, becoming local dignitaries. Different groups of people with different identities and cultural backgrounds met and associated with each other in Quanzhou, making the city a center of different cultures and a world-class oriental city in the Song and Yuan Dynasties. At the same time, they also made Quanzhou a highly internationally-oriented commercial society. These achievements not only promoted the overall prosperity of Quanzhou and made it a center of world trade ports, but also left unique and brilliant multicultural historical sites in Quanzhou.

Quanzhou, a beautiful port city surrounded by erythrina flowers, the official city flower, is renowned overseas as Zaitun or Zayton (another name for ancient Quanzhou). If you stroll through the streets or alleys of this ancient city, you will find temples here and there. In Quanzhou, various religions and different ethnic groups meet and coexist harmoniously, preserving the historical memory of human navigation and trade activities before the Age of Discovery.

天潢贵胄，南外宗人——
南外宗正司遗址

The Site of the Southern Clan Office: Royal Lineage from the Southern Clan Office

南外宗正司遗址外景图。（李芸生 摄）
The exterior view of the Site of the Southern Clan Office. (Photo by Li Yunsheng)

泉州南外宗正司是南宋对迁居泉州的南外皇族群体进行管理的机构。遗址位于泉州鲤城区古榕巷 60 号院内，其北为原城市主干道西街，东侧靠近原城市行政中心子城。作为宋代管理南外宗室人员的官署遗址，泉州南外宗正司由芙蓉堂、天宝池、惩劝所、自新斋、忠厚坊等建筑构成。

南宋皇族群体是泉州世界性多元社群中具有影响力的组成部分，其管理机构在泉州的设置使泉州超越一般的州级地方城市和其他设市舶司的城市，获得较高的政治地位以及较多的政策优待和发展资源，进一步强化了国家政权对泉州海洋贸易的推动及其发展，对泉州社会的发展具有多方面的积极作用及影响。

宋朝立国之初，为避免前朝宗室干预朝政作乱之祸，朝廷给予宗室较为优厚的生活待遇，同时逐步建立制度来限制宗室的权力。其基本原则主要是“优之以爵禄”和“不责以事权”，也即授予宗室成员以虚衔和厚禄，但不给予实权。

南宋朝廷偏安杭州，享国 152 年。（视觉中国 供图）
The Southern Song imperial court was located in Hangzhou, ruling for 152 years. (Courtesy of VCG.COM)

Quanzhou Southern Clan Office was an institution for the management of the southern imperial clans migrating in Quanzhou in the Southern Song Dynasty (1127—1279) . The site is located in the courtyard at No. 60 Gurong Lane, Licheng District, Quanzhou. To its north is the West Street, the former main urban road, and its eastern side is close to Zicheng, the former administrative center. As the site of the government administrative agency, Quanzhou Southern Clan Office consists of buildings such as Furong Hall, Tianbao Pond, Punishment House, Rehabilitation Chamber and Zhonghou Lane.

The Southern Song imperial clan was an influential component of the cosmopolitan and diversified community in Quanzhou. The establishment of Quanzhou Southern Clan Office helped Quanzhou get a higher political status and granted it more policy preferences and development resources compared with other prefectural-level cities and port cities with maritime trade offices, which further strengthened the national government's promotion and the development of Quanzhou's maritime trade. This has made a significant difference to the development of Quanzhou society in many aspects.

In order to avoid interference in political affairs and rebellions by the imperial clans that had occurred in previous dynasties, the imperial court granted the imperial clans relatively favorable living conditions while gradually establishing systems to limit their power in the early days of the founding of the Song Dynasty. Its basic principle was mainly to confer honorary titles and substantial emoluments on them, but not to entrust them with real power.

靖康之变，北宋灭亡。为躲避金兵的追击，同时保存宗室的有生力量，赵宋皇族一路南逃，最终在临安府（今杭州）站稳脚跟。时称“行在所”的临安也由此成为南宋的都城。当时，陆续有部分皇族群体入闽避乱，朝廷顺势将西外宗正司改设于福州，南外宗正司则移司于泉州。这也成为影响福建历史进程的重要事件，为南宋福建的社会经济发展以及文化交流等方面提供新的契机。

1130 年，南宋皇族成员 349 人迁居泉州。至 1233 年，泉州的皇族成员扩至 2,314 人，百年间人口增长近 7 倍。他们广泛参与泉州各项社会事务与海洋贸易，同时也是海外舶来奢侈品的主要消费群体，在一定程度上带动了泉州进口商品的消费需求。

宋元易代之际，蒙古铁骑南下，临安失陷，当时在泉州的南宋宗室遭受“景炎之变”的严重冲击。蒲寿庚献城降元，南外宗子罹难者达三千余人，此为南外宗室自靖康之变后的又一次大劫难，当时只有极少数宦游于外及外逃者幸免于难。在这次劫难中，规模宏大的南外宗正司以及宗人住所睦宗院亦遭焚毁，令人扼腕叹息。明代史学家何乔远在回顾这段历史时亦颇为感慨：“宋家南外刺桐新，凤凰台榭冢麒麟。至今十万编民满，时有当年龙种人。”

The Jingkang Incident in 1127 led to the fall of the Northern Song Dynasty. In order to escape the pursuit of the armies of Jin State while preserving the vitality of the imperial clan, the Zhao-surnamed imperial clan fled to the south. They eventually settled in Lin'an Prefecture (Hangzhou nowadays), a temporary imperial residence at that time, which eventually became the capital of the Southern Song Dynasty. At that time, some members of the royal family fled to Fujian to seek refuge in succession. The imperial court thus relocated the Western Clan Office to Fuzhou and moved the Southern Clan Office to Quanzhou, which was an important event that influenced the historical process of Fujian and provided new opportunities for the social, economic development and cultural exchanges of Fujian in the Southern Song Dynasty.

在泉州海外交通史博物馆中展出的“宋宗室四学士墓”碑为明代进士赵秉孜为宋南外宗室赵由钝之父赵孟襄所立。（成冬冬 摄）

The monument inscribed with "The Tomb of Four Imperial Scholars in the Song Dynasty" on display at Quanzhou Maritime Museum was built by Zhao Bingzi in the Ming Dynasty for Zhao Mengxiang, the father of Zhao Youdun, a member of the Southern Clan in the Song Dynasty. (Photo by Cheng Dongdong)

The number of imperial clansmen in the Southern Song Dynasty living in Quanzhou surged from 349 in 1130 to 2,314 in 1233, a nearly seven-fold increase in a century. They participated widely in various social affairs and maritime trade in Quanzhou, and were the main consumers for luxuries imported from overseas, which to some extent drove the demand for consumption of imported goods in Quanzhou.

During the transition from the Song Dynasty to the Yuan Dynasty, the Mongol empire advanced southward and captured Lin'an. At that time, the Southern Song imperial family in Quanzhou suffered greatly due to the Jingyan Incident. Pu Shougeng, a merchant and then the chief of the Maritime Trade Office in the Southern Song Dynasty, surrendered the city to the Yuan army, and more than three thousand members of the Southern Clan were killed. This was another catastrophe for the Southern Clan after the Jingkang Incident. Only a very small number of the clansmen who had been officials in other places or who had already fled survived. In the calamity, it was such a pity for all the buildings of the Southern Clan Office and the residence of the imperial clansmen were burned down. He Qiaoyuan, a historian in the Ming Dynasty (1368—1644), sighed whilst reminiscing about the history, "Erythrina blooms where Southern Song's imperials once dwelled, beneath grand mansions their tombs in silent farewell. The populance now counts a hundred thousand households anew, and quite some flow the royal blood."

南外宗正司移司泉州事实上推动了泉州在宋代经济、社会、文化等方面的发展。（李芸生 摄）
The relocation of the Southern Clan Office to Quanzhou promoted the development of Quanzhou's economy, society, culture and other aspects in the Song Dynasty. (Photo by Li Yunsheng)

南外宗正司的由来与职能

赵宋立国之初，沿袭唐代的做法设立宗正寺作为管理宗室的机构，负责编修皇族属籍及人口呈报等事务。随着宗室人口不断繁衍增加，宋仁宗于景祐三年（1036）设立大宗正司，并在宗室成员中遴选位高属尊者为判大宗正事。为明晰宗正寺与大宗正司的职权，朝廷还对两个机构的职能做了分工，“凡宗室事，大宗正司治之；玉牒之类，宗正寺掌之”。

为了缓解都城开封宗人的居住情况，又于崇宁元年至崇宁三年（1102—1104）在南京应天府（今河南商丘）设置南外宗正司，在西京河南府（今河南洛阳）设置西外宗正司。

建于北宋皇宫遗址之上的开封龙亭公园。（视觉中国 供图）
Kaifeng Longting Park built on the site of the royal palace of the Northern Song Dynasty. (Courtesy of VCG.COM)

宋代宗室管理机构职能分解表

<table>
<tr><th>机构名称</th><th>宗正寺</th><th>大宗正司</th><th>南外宗正司</th><th>西外宗正司</th></tr>
<tr><td>设置时间</td><td>建隆元年（960）</td><td>景祐三年（1036）</td><td colspan="2">崇宁元年至崇宁三年（1102—1104）</td></tr>
<tr><td rowspan="2">机构职能</td><td rowspan="2">主要负责帝王宗庙、诸陵的荐享祭祀以及修纂、保管皇族属籍等事务</td><td>表率宗室，纠合族属</td><td colspan="2">负责管理地方宗室事务</td></tr>
<tr><td colspan="3">制定皇属内赏罚法令规式，对违犯宗人训诫惩处；
兼管宗室教育；
负责宗室赐名授官、磨勘迁转、袭封赠官等事宜；
办理宗室陈乞请给、发放嫁娶房奁、赈恤孤遗贫乏、分配财产等经济事务</td></tr>
</table>

The Origin and Functions of the Southern Clan Office

In the early years of the Northern Song Dynasty, the imperial court followed the tradition in the Tang Dynasty and established the Royal Clan Office as the institution to manage imperial clans, which was responsible for compiling the genealogy and population registration of imperial clans. With the continuous growth of the imperial clan population, Emperor Renzong, the fourth emperor of the Song Dynasty, set up the Grand Clan Office in 1036, and selected senior and respectable members from imperial clans to handle the affairs. To clarify the division of authority between the two institutions, the imperial court also defined their functions: "All affairs regarding imperial clans should be handled by the Grand Clan Office, while the genealogy about the members of imperial clans should be in the charge of the Royal Clan Office."

In order to provide imperial clan members in Kaifeng (the capital city then) with more living space, the imperial court established the Southern Clan Office in Yingtian Prefecture (Shangqiu in Henan Province nowadays) and the Western Clan Office in Henan Prefecture (Luoyang in Henan Province nowadays) in the period of 1102 to 1104.

Table of Functions of Imperial Clan Management Institutions in the Song Dynasty

<table>
<tr><th>Name</th><th>Royal Clan Office</th><th>Grand Clan Office</th><th>Southern Clan Office</th><th>Western Clan Office</th></tr>
<tr><td>Establishment Time</td><td>960</td><td>1036</td><td colspan="2">1102—1104</td></tr>
<tr><td rowspan="2">Functions</td><td rowspan="2">To be responsible for sacrificial rituals of emperors' ancestral temples and their mausoleums; compilation and preservation of genealogy and records of the imperial clan</td><td>To be an example for the imperial clansmen and unite its members</td><td colspan="2">To manage the affairs of local imperial clan</td></tr>
<tr><td colspan="3">To formulate laws and regulations regarding rewards and punishments for the imperial clan, and discipline and punish those who violate the rules;
To be responsible for the education of the imperial clan members;
To be responsible for bestowing names and titles, job assignments and transfers, and conferring noble titles on the imperial clan members;
To handle funds and resources requested by the imperial clan members in their petitions, provide dowries and housing subsidies for newly-married imperial clan members, relief subsidies and aid to impoverished imperial clan members, and distribute and allocate properties</td></tr>
</table>

朱熹像。（闽人 供图）
Portrait of Zhu Xi (1130—1200), a Neo-Confucian philosopher of the Southern Song Dynasty. (Courtesy of Minren)

朱熹在与其弟子谈到“漳泉宗室最多”的原因时指出，“南外、西外，在彼宫中不能容，则皆出居于外”，“徽宗以宗室众多，京师不能容，故令秦王位下子孙出居西京，谓之‘西外’；太祖位下子孙出居南京，谓之‘南外’。及靖康之乱，遭虏人杀戮掳掠之余，能渡江自全者，高宗亦遣州郡收拾。于是皆分置福泉二州，依旧分太祖、秦王位下而居之也。居于京师者，皆太宗以下子孙”。

从上述朱熹的话语中可知，南外宗正司最初是管理宋太祖赵匡胤位下子孙，因驻地在南京应天府而被称为“南外”；西外宗正司则是管理秦王赵廷美位下子孙，因设在西京河南府而谓之“西外”。然而，随着南迁避乱以及后来宗人间的仕宦交游，实际上居住在福州与泉州的宗室，已没有特别明晰的界限，其中也不乏太宗派下子孙。

When discussing with his disciples the reason why most Southern Clan members lived in Zhangzhou and Quanzhou, Zhu Xi pointed out that "the Southern and Western royal lineages could not be accommodated in the imperial palace, so they had to live in other places." "During the reign of Emperor Huizong in the Song Dynasty, there were too many imperial family members, so the imperial capital could not accommodate them all. He ordered the descendants of King Qin (Zhao Tingmei, the fourth younger brother of Emperor Taizu) to reside in Xijing (the Western Capital, today's Luoyang), calling them the 'Western Lineages', and the descendants of Emperor Taizu (Zhao Kuangyin, the founder and the first emperor of the Song Dynasty) to reside in Nanjing (the Southern Capital, today's Shangqiu), calling them the 'Southern Lineages'. After the Jingkang Incident, the survivors of royal family from the massacres and abductions of the Jurchen who could cross the Yangtze River were taken in by the local governments upon Emperor Gaozong's command. They were allocated to either Fuzhou or Quanzhou according to whether they were descendants of Emperor Taizu or King Qin, while those dwelling in the capital were all descendants of Emperor Taizong."

According to Zhu Xi, the Southern Clan Office was originally established to manage the descendants of Emperor Taizu of the Song Dynasty. As their residence was Yingtian Prefecture (the southern capital at that time, referring to today's Shangqiu in Henan Province), it was called "Southern (Clan)". The Western Clan Office was established to manage the descendants of King Qin. As their residence was Henan Prefecture (the western capital at that time, today's Luoyang in Henan Province), it was called "Western (Clan)". However, because of the southward migration to avoid wars and the interactions between kinsmen, the royal lineage living in Fuzhou and Quanzhou had no clear boundaries, including descendants of Emperor Taizong.

南外宗人的入泉路线、时间

靖康二年（1127），金兵南下攻取开封，宋徽宗与宋钦宗被掳北上。五月初一日，宋徽宗第九子、宋钦宗的异母弟康王赵构在南京应天府即皇帝位，改年号为建炎，是为宋高宗。在宋室不断南迁过程中，两外宗正司亦随之流转。

南外宗正司遗址陈列馆内景。（李芸生 摄）

The interior view of the exhibition hall on the site of the Southern Clan Office. (Photo by Li Yunsheng)

The Route and Time of the Members of the Southern Clan Entering Quanzhou

In 1127, the armies of the Jin State invaded the Northern Song empire and captured Kaifeng, the capital city. Emperor Huizong and Emperor Qinzong were taken as captives. On the first day of lunar May, King Kang Zhao Gou, the ninth son of Emperor Huizong and half-brother of Emperor Qinzong, ascended the throne in Nanjing (the Southern Capital, today's Shangqiu), changing the era name to Jianyan and becoming Emperor Gaozong of the Song Dynasty. During the successive southward migrations of the imperial court, the two clan offices followed accordingly.

据《宋史》记载，当时的大宗正司移至江宁（今南京）；西外宗正司则经扬州转至福州；南外宗正司初由河南应天府经镇江，中间或许还在明州（今宁波）有过短暂停留，其前期准备由朝廷先在泉、福两地招募闽、广海舟，再由知南外宗正事赵士樽率领，自镇江经海路而至泉州。

关于南外宗正司移置泉州的时间，有建炎初、建炎三年底（1129）、绍兴元年（1131）、绍兴三年（1133）多种说法。参考福州西外宗正司的设立过程，建炎三年底应是宗人初来泉州的时间，为及时处理宗人事务，当时该司尚属暂设机构，不过，随着宗人逐渐在福州、泉州定居下来，临设机构由虚转实，因此绍兴三年应该是南外宗正司在泉州正式确立的时间。

According to *The History of Song*, at that time, the Grand Clan Office was moved to Jiangning (Nanjing nowadays). The Western Clan Office was moved to Yangzhou and then to Fuzhou. The Southern Clan Office from Yingtian Prefecture, was moved to Zhenjiang, and finally to Quanzhou. In the process, the office might stop in Mingzhou (Ningbo nowadays) temporarily. In the early preparation, the imperial court recruited the vessels from Fujian and Guangdong in Quanzhou and Fuzhou, and then Zhao Shizun, the Minister of the Southern Clan Office, led the office to move from Zhenjiang to Quanzhou via the sea route.

The relocation of the Southern Clan Office to Quanzhou may begin in 1127, the end of 1129, 1131, or 1133 AD. Taking the Western Clan Office's establishment process in Fuzhou as a reference, the time when the clansmen first came to Quanzhou should be in the end of 1129. At that time, to handle the affairs of the clansmen timely, the agency was still a provisional one. However, with the clansmen gradually settling down in Fuzhou and Quanzhou, the provisional agency became an office finally, so 1133 AD should be the time when the Southern Clan Office was formally established in Quanzhou.

放生池·水陆院·南外宗正司

泉州南外宗正司所处方位，位于肃清门西南、开元寺以南。据成书于明代的《八闽通志》“南外宗正司”条载：“在府治西南忠厚坊……元改为清源驿，今为织染局。”查“清源驿”条，我们看到元代的清源驿是由南外宗正司改建而成，而南外宗正司的附属建筑在经历宋元之变后，也只剩下惩劝所与自新斋，明代时此处则被改为织染局。

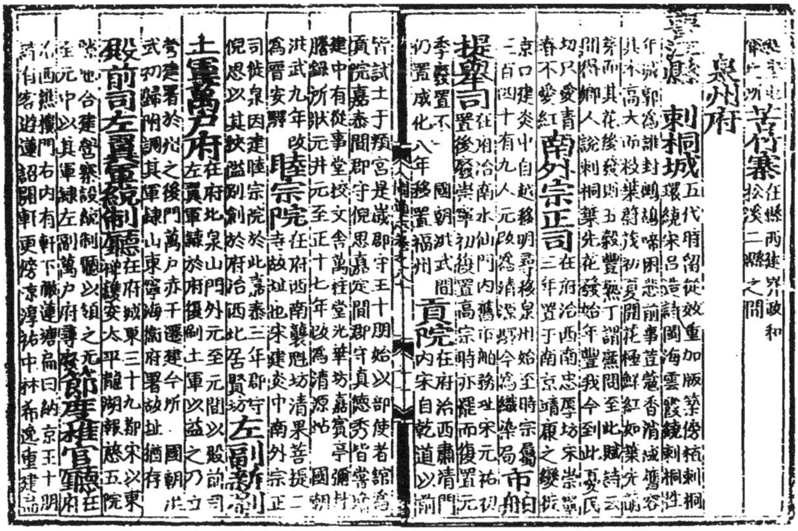

《八闽通志》卷之八十“古迹”南外宗正司书影。（林瀚 供图）

The Southern Clan Office in Volume 80 of General Gazetteer of Fujian. (Courtesy of Lin Han)

Free Life Pond, Water-Land Institute and the Southern Clan Office

Quanzhou Southern Clan Office was to the southeast of Suqing Gate and to the south of Kaiyuan Temple. According to the entry of “the Southern Clan Office” from *General Gazetteer of Fujian* compiled in the Ming Dynasty, “It was located in Zhonghou Lane in the southwest of Quanzhou Prefecture... Then it was changed into Qingyuan Courtier Station during the Yuan Dynasty, and now it is the Weaving and Dyeing Bureau.” According to the entry “Qingyuan Courtier Station”, it can be seen that Qingyuan Courtier Station in the Yuan Dynasty was rebuilt based on the Southern Clan Office. After the Song-Yuan dynastic transition, all the attached buildings of the Southern Clan Office except for Punishment House and Rehabilitation Chamber were ruined. Thus, Quanzhou Southern Clan Office was changed into the Weaving and Dyeing Bureau in the Ming Dynasty.

通过对明清方志的梳理可知，南外宗正司所处的这片区域，在唐天宝六年（747）时为祝圣放生池，周回四里，后于池上建水陆堂，乾符六年（879）为护国水陆院，到北宋时仍然是作为寺院在使用；此后又被改为都监廨舍和添差通判厅。南宋建炎年间宋室皇族迁来泉州后，此地改为南外宗正司。就其建筑布局来看，内有惩劝所、自新斋、芙蓉堂及池、天宝池、忠厚坊诸胜。像惩劝所、自新斋的命名和设置，显然是为了管理宗人，使之遵纪守法，同时也有提醒宗室成员引以为戒、悔过自新之意。

宋元变革，战祸再起，蒲寿庚在泉州城屠杀南外宗室三千。此后南外宗正司所在地屡有更易。元代曾于此处设清源驿，同时还有部分区域被复建为禅院；明代为水陆寺，明正统三年（1438）又将其部分改为织染局。此后，御史汪旦又废寺为宅，水陆寺被迁往开元寺西偏。现南外宗正司的相关建筑早已堙没，多半为民居所占，只剩水池稍有残存。

赵氏皇族除了在泉州设置南外宗正司外，还设立了睦宗院及宗学等相关机构。宋亡之后，睦宗院等机构演变为泉州天源赵氏的祠堂等场所，留下“犀牛望月”的地名传说和“乡贤名宦”木匾等遗存。

现移往开元寺内的水陆寺。（成冬冬 摄）
Water-Land Temple moved into Kaiyuan Temple now. (Photo by Cheng Dongdong)

Based on a review of local chronicles of the Ming and Qing Dynasties, it is known that in 747 of the Tang Dynasty, the area where the Southern Clan Office was located was Free Life Pond for consecration, with a circumference of four *li* (approximately 2,000 meters), and the Water-Land Hall was built over the pond. In 879, it became Water-Land Institute for national safety. During the Northern Song Dynasty, it was still being used as a temple. Afterwards, it was changed into the government office of the central inspectorate dispatched to the local area and temporary officials assigned there. From 1127 to 1130 of the Southern Song Dynasty, this place was changed into the Southern Clan Office after the Song imperial clansmen relocated in Quanzhou. In terms of its architectural layout, there were Punishment House, Rehabilitation Chamber, Furong Hall, Furong Pond, Tianbao Pond, Zhonghou Lane and others. Obviously, the naming and establishment of places like Punishment House and Rehabilitation Chamber were meant to manage the imperial clan members and force them to abide by the rules, while also reminding them of self-reflection.

In the transition from the Song Dynasty to the Yuan Dynasty, wars broke out. Pu Shougeng massacred 3,000 members of the Southern Clan in Quanzhou. Since then, the location of the Southern Clan Office had been used for different purposes repeatedly. During the Yuan Dynasty, Qingyuan Courtier Station was set up here, and part of the area was rebuilt as a temple. During the Ming Dynasty, it was changed into Water-Land Temple, and in 1438, part of it was changed into Weaving and Dyeing Bureau. Afterwards, the censor Wang Dan turned the temple into a residence, and Water-Land Temple was moved to the west side of Kaiyuan Temple. Nowadays, the relevant buildings of the Southern Clan Office have long been abandoned, and most of them are occupied by private houses, with only the pool remaining.

In addition to the Southern Clan Office, Zhao-surnamed imperial clansmen also established Muzong Institute, a clan school, and other institutions in Quanzhou. After the demise of the Song Dynasty, Muzong Institute became the ancestral hall of Quanzhou's Zhao-surnamed Tianyuan clansmen, leaving behind a legend about the place name "Rhinoceros Gazing at the Moon", a wooden plaque inscribed with characters "Country Worthy and Eminent Official" and other relics.

“乡贤名宦”木匾。（李芸生 摄）
The wooden plaque inscribed with the Chinese characters "乡贤名宦" (Country Worthy and Eminent Official). (Photo by Li Yunsheng)

泉州南外宗正司遗址的考古发现

2019 年，中国社会科学院考古研究所、福建博物院、泉州市海上丝绸之路申遗中心联合组成泉州城考古工作队，对南外宗正司遗址进行考古勘探和发掘，勘探面积约 1,400 平方米，由此也为我们揭开泉州南外宗正司的神秘面纱。

2019 年、2020 年，考古人员分两次对泉州南外宗正司遗址进行考古发掘，揭露出三处台基建筑基址，一处建筑基址，一处水池的东、南岸线等遗迹。这些遗迹的揭露，为复原天宝池、水陆院及南外宗正司提供重要的考古依据。

在遗址中还先后出土了“官”字砖、脊兽和兽首饰件、兽面纹和十九瓣莲花纹瓦当等官署建筑构件。从瓦当纹样来看，也与杭州、洛阳等地宋代重要官式建筑遗址中发现的瓦当纹样相近，这也进一步佐证该组建筑为宋代官方营建的较高等级官署建筑。

南外宗正司遗址考古现场航拍图。（成冬冬　摄）
An aerial photo of the archaeological site of the Southern Clan Office. (Photo by Cheng Dongdong)

Archaeological Findings at the Site of the Southern Clan Office in Quanzhou

In 2019, an archaeological team formed by the Institute of Archaeology of the Chinese Academy of Sciences, Fujian Museum, and Quanzhou's World Heritage Application Center of Maritime Silk Road conducted archaeological surveys and excavations at the site of the Southern Clan Office. It was found that the office covered an area of approximately 1,400 square meters. This finding uncovered the mysterious veil over the Southern Clan Office in Quanzhou.

Furthermore, the team conducted two excavations at the site of the Southern Clan Office in Quanzhou in 2019 and 2020 respectively. They unearthed three sites of foundations of platform-based buildings, one building foundation, the east and south embankments of a pool and other ruins, which provided important archaeological references for the restoration of Tianbao Pond, Water-Land Institute and the Southern Clan Office.

Besides, architectural components of official buildings have been unearthed successively on the site, including bricks inscribed with the character "Guan" (official), animal-shaped roof-ridge and animal head architectural ornaments, eave tiles with animal masks and eave tiles with nineteen-petal lotus pattern, etc. The patterns of the eave tiles are similar to those found at important official architectural sites of the Song Dynasty in Hangzhou, Luoyang and other places, which further proves that these buildings are official buildings at a relatively high level built in the Song Dynasty.

南外宗正司遗址出土的“官”字砖、“官”字板瓦、兽首饰件及十九瓣莲花纹瓦当。（成冬冬 摄）
Bricks and flat roof tiles inscribed with the character "Guan" (official), animal head architectural ornaments and eave tiles with nineteen-petal lotus pattern unearthed from the site of the Southern Clan Office. (Photo by Cheng Dongdong)

根据考古研究发现，泉州古城在唐宋两代的布局方向上存在差异。唐代泉州城的建筑及路网是以开元寺大雄宝殿的中轴线为参照，约呈正南正北方向；宋代以降的泉州城建筑及路网，则以东西塔连线的垂线为参照。根据历史文献记载，南外宗正司内的部分建筑可能源自唐代建于池上的水陆堂。在发掘区西侧的建筑基址方向近南北向，建于水中台地之上，出土有大量莲花纹、芙蓉纹瓦当，可能为宋代芙蓉堂所在，并可能与唐代水陆堂等建筑有关。

而在发掘区东侧，建筑基址方向为南偏西 9 度，则应是南宋时期南外宗正司所见其他建筑基址。南外宗正司遗址的建筑基址与泉州城不同历史时期的布局方向紧密关联，显示出宋元泉州城北部行政性城区的布局特征。

考古人员根据揭露出来的建筑遗迹，推测了南外宗正司遗址相关水池遗迹的范围约为东西 94 米、南北 133 米，南外宗正司的四至范围依水池四边各延伸 50 米，即约东西 194 米、南北 233 米，据此推断当时南外宗正司的占地面积约 45,000 平方米。

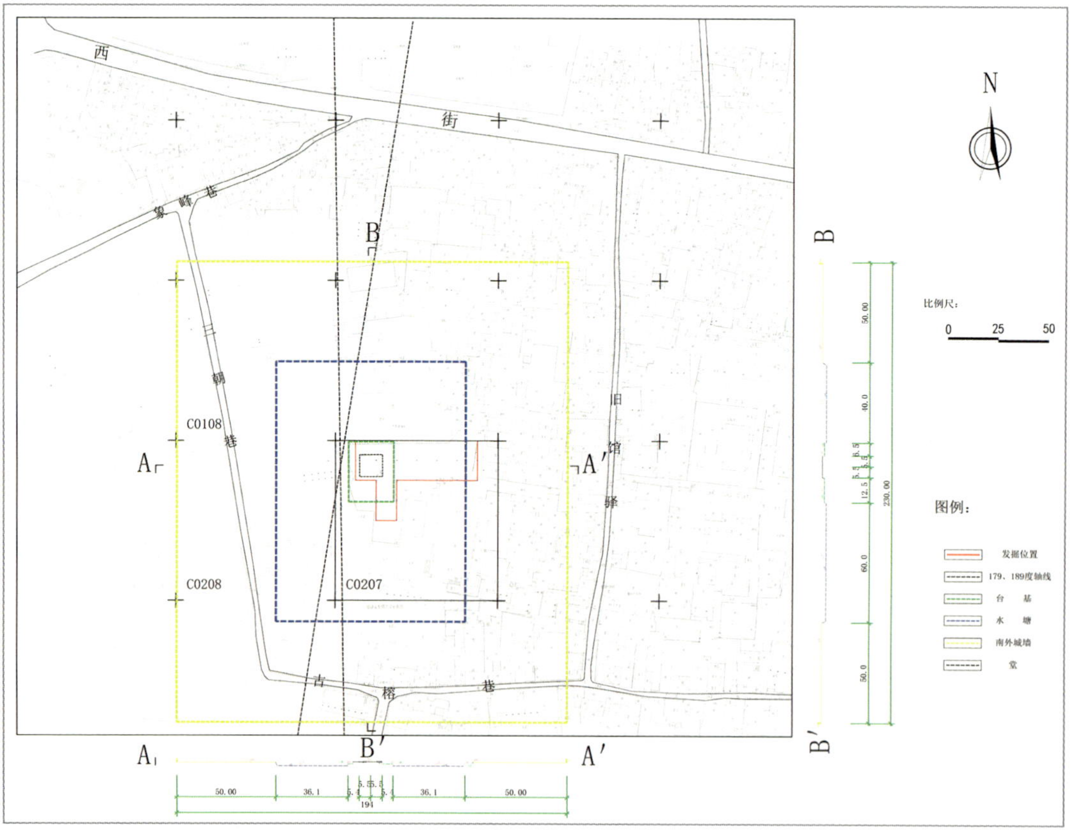

泉州南外宗正司遗址四至及相关水池遗迹范围复原示意图。（泉州市文物考古研究所 供图）

The restoration illustration of the scope of the site of Quanzhou Southern Clan Office and the related pool. (Courtesy of Quanzhou Institute of Archaeology)

The archaeological research found that there existed differences in the layout orientation between the Tang and Song Dynasties in Quanzhou. The architecture and road network of Quanzhou in the Tang Dynasty faced roughly the south, which referred to the central axis of Mahavira Hall of Kaiyuan Temple. Since the Song Dynasty, they faced the east, referring to the vertical lines connecting East Pagoda and West Pagoda. According to historical records, some buildings in the Southern Clan Office may have originated from Water-Land Hall built on the pool in the Tang Dynasty. The foundations of these buildings in the western part of the excavation site faced roughly the south, built on a platform above water. Furthermore, a large number of eave tiles with lotus pattern and hibiscus pattern were unearthed from these building remains. Therefore, the site might be the location of Furong Hall in the Song Dynasty and be related to the buildings including Water-Land Hall in the Tang Dynasty.

In the east side of the excavation site, the foundations face the south by west at 9 degrees, which might be the foundations of other buildings of the Southern Clan Office in the Southern Song Dynasty. The building foundations of the Southern Clan Office are closely related to the layout orientations of Quanzhou in different historical periods, showing the layout characteristics of the administrative district in the northern part of Quanzhou during the Song and Yuan Dynasties.

Based on the exposed architectural relics, archaeologists estimated that the scope of the pool ruins related to the site of Quanzhou Southern Clan Office was about 94 meters in the east-west direction and 133 meters in the north-south direction. If extending 50 meters from each side of the pool, it could be estimated that Quanzhou Southern Clan Office had covered an area of about 194 meters in the east-west direction and 233 meters in the north-south direction with a total area of about 45,000 square meters.

南外宗正司遗址出土瓷器按釉色分为青瓷、白（青白）瓷、黑（酱）瓷、青花瓷、素胎器等，器形主要有碗、盏、碟、杯、盘、盆、罐、执壶、瓶、粉盒、灯盏、炉等，涉及的窑口有泉州地区的磁灶窑、东门窑、安溪窑、德化窑、南安窑等，福建其他地区的有漳平永福窑、云霄水头窑、闽清义窑、福清东张窑、武夷山遇林亭窑、建阳建窑等，福建以外的有浙江龙泉窑和越窑、陕西耀州窑、河北定窑、江西景德镇窑等。从这些丰富的窑口瓷器可看出泉州是当时全国瓷器的重要转运中心与消费市场。

在出土的陶瓷器中，还发现涉及机构名称的“水陆”“水六库司”“宗厨”等墨书，佐证了此处曾与水陆堂（院）、南外宗正司等机构相关。除此之外，还有“天王”“西塔”“癸亥酱坊置”“玲房”“殿司”等墨书，这些或也与开元寺的天王殿、西塔以及周边酱坊商铺等有关。

另外值得注意的还有如“赵”姓，以及涉及人名的“允”“叔”“仲”“彦”“宗”“崇”等墨书器底。这些字多为赵宋皇族的辈分字，是与皇族群体有关的重要线索，这也进一步佐证了遗址位置和建筑遗迹性质。

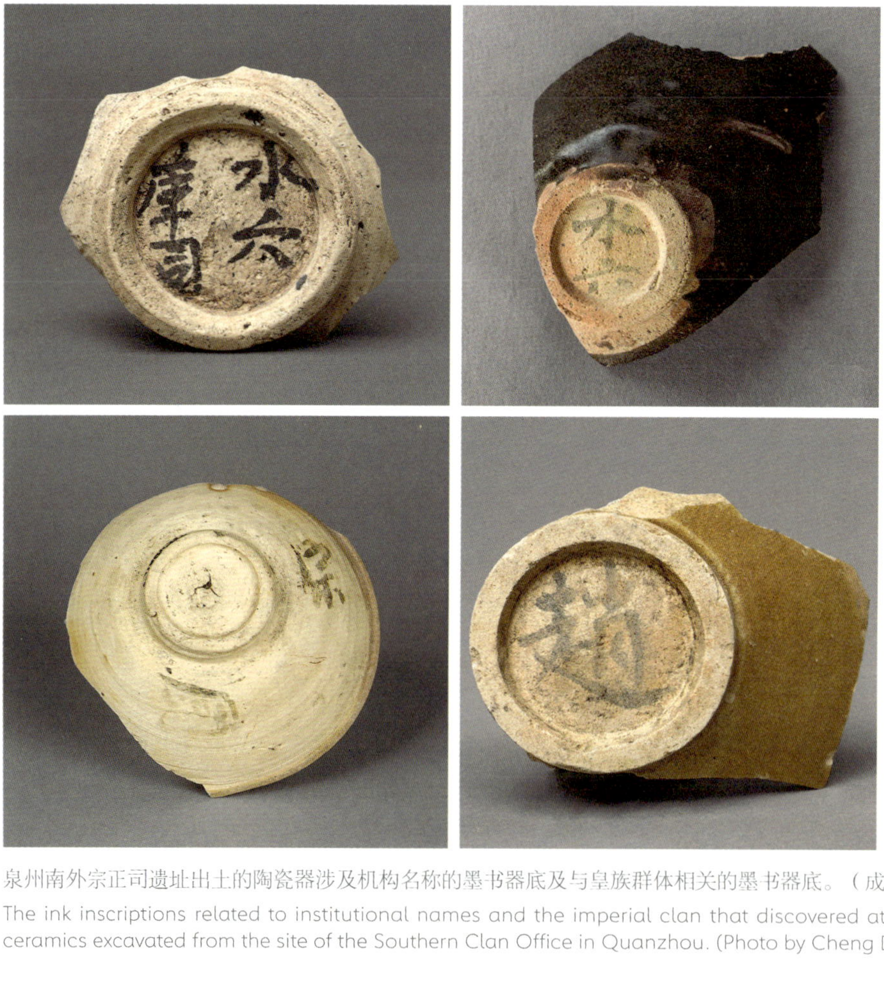

泉州南外宗正司遗址出土的陶瓷器涉及机构名称的墨书器底及与皇族群体相关的墨书器底。（成冬冬 摄）
The ink inscriptions related to institutional names and the imperial clan that discovered at the bottom of the ceramics excavated from the site of the Southern Clan Office in Quanzhou. (Photo by Cheng Dongdong)

According to glaze colors, the unearthed ceramic wares can be classified into celadon, white (bluish-white), black (caramel-color), blue-and-white glazed porcelain wares and unglazed pottery. In terms of shape, there are bowls, calices, plates, cups, dishes, basins, vases, ewers, bottles, powder boxes, oil lamps, stoves, etc. The kilns involved are Cizao Kilns, Dongmen Kilns, Anxi Kilns, Dehua Kilns, and Nan'an Kilns in Quanzhou. In other areas of Fujian, there are Yongfu Kilns in Zhangping, Shuitou Kilns in Yunxiao, Yi Kilns in Minqing, Dongzhang Kilns in Fuqing, Yulinting Kilns in Wuyishan, and Jian Kilns in Jianyang. Kilns outside Fujian include Longquan Kilns and Yue Kilns in Zhejiang, Yaozhou Kilns in Shaanxi, Ding Kilns in Hebei, and Jingdezhen Kilns in Jiangxi. It can be seen that Quanzhou was an important center for transshipment and consumer market of ceramics in China at that time.

Among the unearthed ceramics, inscriptions related to institutional names such as "Water-Land", "Water-Land Administrative Office" and "Chef of Imperial Clan" were discovered, corroborating that this site was once associated with institutions such as Water-Land Hall (or Water-Land Institute) and the Southern Clan Office. In addition, there are also such inscriptions as "Heavenly King", "West Pagoda", "Purchased by Sauce Shop in Guihai Year", "Ling's Workshop" and "Palace Ministry", which may also be related to the Devaraja Hall, West Pagoda of Kaiyuan Temple and sauce workshops around it.

Besides, it's worth noting that there are ink inscriptions at the bottom of utensils with the "Zhao" surname, and names including "Yun", "Shu", "Zhong", "Yan", "Zong" and "Chong". Many of these characters are generation names of the Zhao-surnamed imperial clans in the Song Dynasty, which are important clues related to the imperial clan. This further corroborates the relations between the location of the site and the architectural ruins.

南宋宗室在泉州的生活及影响

随着南宋皇族入泉，宗室群体不仅参与泉州的地方政治生活，而且对当地经济消费升级、丝织工艺提升、戏曲文化传播等方面都起到重要的推动作用。泉州南外宗室人员积极参与科举，入仕为官人数众多，极大提升宗室在泉州的政治影响力。作为皇族群体，他们广泛参与泉州各项社会事务与海洋贸易，极大地刺激了泉州的高端消费市场和贸易需求，进一步促进泉州海内外贸易的繁荣发展。他们的到来大幅提升了泉州本地的消费能力，特别是他们对香药、珍宝等高端舶来品的消费刺激了进口需求。宗人之中还有一些人担任了地方政府和市舶司官员，他们参与港口建设和商贸管理，为海洋贸易和港口发展发挥积极作用；有些甚至作为商人直接参与海洋贸易。在九日山的祈风活动中就有许多是赵氏宗人。此外，宗人们还参与泉州府文庙、安平桥等地方设施的修建活动，推动了泉州地域文化的发展与转变。

1974 年泉州后渚港发现的宋代沉船上曾出土木质牌签 96 件，其中 19 件标有“南家”，8 件标有“安郡”“河郡”“兆郡”“昶郡”等字。有研究者认为这些牌签表明该船的贸易活动有南外宗正司及宗室人员参与，显示出宋元泉州浓厚的商业氛围。

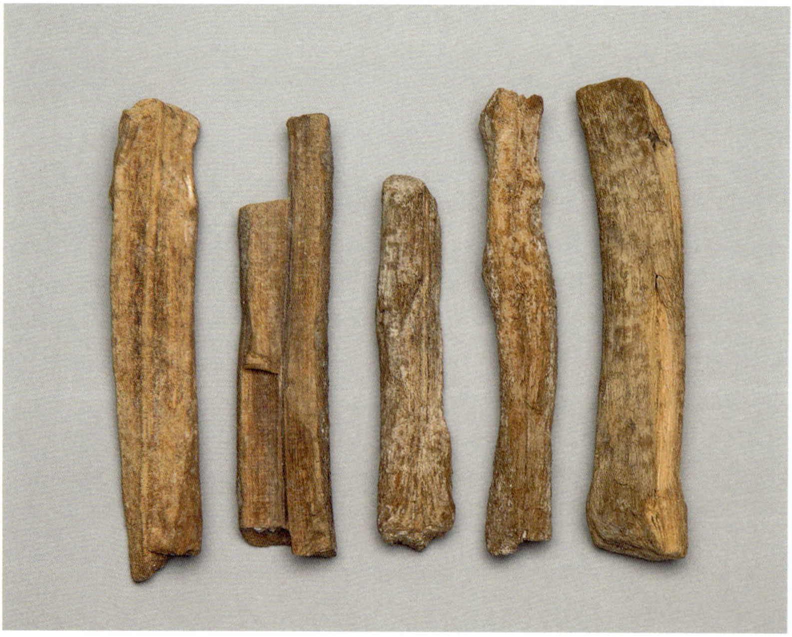

泉州后渚港宋代沉船出土香料。（成冬冬 摄）
The incense wood unearthed from the sunken ship in the Song Dynasty in Houzhu Harbor in Quanzhou. (Photo by Cheng Dongdong)

The Life of the Imperial Clan Members and Their Influence on Quanzhou in the Southern Song Dynasty

With the entry of the Southern Song imperial clansmen into Quanzhou, they not only participated in Quanzhou's local political life, but also played an important role in the upgrade of economic consumption, the improvement of silk fabric craftsmanship, and the spread of opera culture. The success of the members of the Southern Clan in the Imperial Examinations and their subsequent entry into officialdom significantly increased their political influence in Quanzhou. As an imperial clan group, they were widely involved in Quanzhou's various social affairs and maritime trade and greatly boosted Quanzhou's high-end consumer market and trade demands, which further promoted the prosperity of Quanzhou's domestic and foreign trade. Their arrival greatly improved Quanzhou's local consumption capabilities. Especially, their consumption of exotic imported goods like fragrant medicine and treasures stimulated import demand. Of the imperial family members, some also served as the officials in the local government and the maritime trade office, participating in port construction and commercial management, thus playing a positive role in maritime trade and port development. Other clan members even engaged directly in maritime trade as merchants. Many of the participants in the wind-praying ceremonies on Jiuri Mountain were of the Zhao-surnamed clansmen. In addition, the clan members also participated in the construction of local facilities like Confucian Temple in Quanzhou and Anping Bridge, promoting the development and transformation of Quanzhou's local culture.

In 1974, 96 wooden name slips were discovered on a sunken ship found in Houzhu Harbor in Quanzhou. Among them, 19 are marked with the characters "Southern Family", and 8 with such characters as "An Prefecture", "He Prefecture", "Zhao Prefecture", and "Chang Prefecture". Some scholars believe that these name seals indicate that the members of the Southern Clan Office and the imperial clansmen were involved in the trade activities of the ship, showing the vibrant commercial atmosphere of Quanzhou during the Song and Yuan Dynasties.

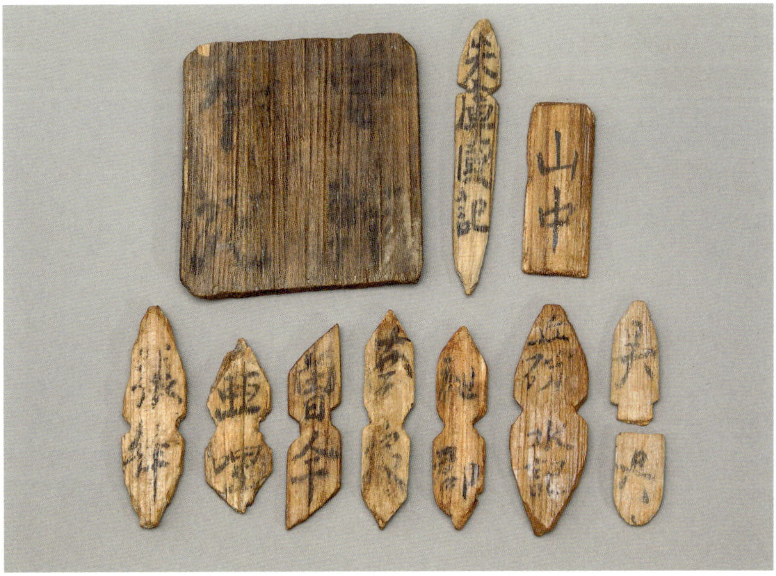

泉州后渚港宋代沉船出土木牌签。（成冬冬 摄）
Wooden name slips unearthed from the sunken ship in the Song Dynasty in Houzhu Harbor in Quanzhou. (Photo by Cheng Dongdong)

泉州九日山上共有九方关于宗室人员参与海外贸易祈风祭典活动的摩崖石刻，他们以市舶司官员、宗正司知宗、郡守等身份主持或参与祈风仪式。

宗室人员参与九日山祈风活动表

序号	摩崖石刻名称	时间	所涉赵氏宗人	位置
1	宋虞仲房等冬季祈风题刻	淳熙元年(1174)，岁在甲午季冬朔	赵德季、赵致孚、赵子张	九日山西峰石刻群南侧中层岩崖间
2	宋司马伋等冬季祈风题刻	淳熙十年(1183)，岁在昭阳单阏，闰月廿有四日	同典宗赵子涛	九日山西峰南麓石刻群下层岩壁间
3	宋林枅等夏冬两季祈风题刻	淳熙戊申(1188)夏四月	赵公迥、赵不遏、赵善䆳	九日山东峰南麓石刻群东侧岩崖间
4	宋章徕等夏季祈风题刻	嘉定癸未(1223)二十日，戊戌	开封赵汝芃千里、三山赵与官清叟、俊仪赵善軿载卿	九日山西峰南麓石刻群下层岩壁间
5	宋颜颐仲等夏季祈风题刻	淳祐癸卯(1243)孟夏乙丑	舶幞赵幕崇𥁕 宗正徽猷赵师恕（适拜开国命，弗果至也）	九日山西峰石刻群南侧下层壁间
6	宋赵师耕等冬季祈风题刻	淳祐丁未(1247)仲冬二十有一日	古汴赵师耕以郡兼舶	九日山西峰石刻群南侧下层壁间
7	宋谢埴等冬季祈风题刻	宝祐丁巳(1257)仲冬下澣	宗正天水赵师淯东之	九日山西峰东麓石刻群南侧上层岩崖间
8	宋方澄孙等夏季祈风题刻	宝祐戊午(1258)四月辛卯	赵时緟	九日山西峰石刻群最北端岩崖间
9	宋赵希怿等冬季祈风题刻	咸淳丙寅(1266)，南至后十日	知宗兼郡事古汴赵希怿安宅、东嘉赵崇东旸卿	九日山西峰东坡“九日山”题刻南侧岩崖间

泉州九日山祈风石刻群。（陈起拓 摄）
The stone inscriptions for wind-praying on Jiuri Mountain in Quanzhou. (Photo by Chen Qituo)

On Jiuri Mountain in Quanzhou, there are nine stone inscriptions related to the imperial clan members participating in wind-praying ceremonies for successful maritime trade. They presided over or participated in the wind-praying ceremonies as the officials in charge of the maritime trade office, ministers of the clan office, or prefects.

List of Participation of the Imperial Clan Members in Wind-Praying Ceremonies on Jiuri Mountain

No.	Name of Inscribed Precipices	Time	The Zhao-surnamed Clan Members Involved	Location of Inscribed Precipices
1	The inscription by Yu Zhongfang and others in winter's wind-praying ceremonies in the Song Dynasty	On the 1st day of lunar December of the 1st year of the Chunxi Period (1174)	Zhao Deji, Zhao Zhifu, and Zhao Zizhang	On the middle cliffs on the southern side of the inscribed rocks at the West Peak of Jiuri Mountain
2	The inscription by Sima Ji and others in winter's wind-praying ceremonies in the Song Dynasty	On the 24th of the leap November of the 10th year of the Chunxi Period (1183)	Zhao Zitao, an official in charge of editing and revising national laws and regulations at the imperial court	On the lower rock walls at the southern foot of the West Peak of Jiuri Mountain
3	The inscription by Lin Ji and others in wind-praying ceremonies in summer and winter in the Song Dynasty	In lunar April of the 15th year of the Chunxi Period (1188)	Zhao Gongjiong, Zhao Buti and Zhao Shanshun	On the eastern cliffs at the southern foot of the East Peak of Jiuri Mountain
4	The inscription by Zhang Lai and others in summer's wind-praying ceremonies in the Song Dynasty	On the 20th day of lunar October of the 16th year of Jiading Period (1223)	Zhao Ruqi, Zhao Yuguan, and Zhao Shanpeng	On the lower rock walls of the inscribed rocks on the southern side of the West Peak of Jiuri Mountain
5	The inscription by Yan Yizhong and others in summer's wind-praying ceremonies in the Song Dynasty	On the day of Yichou in lunar April of the 3rd year of Chunyou Period (1243)	Zhao Mu, Zhao Shishu (he received the order to pay respects to the founding emperor, so did not present the ceremony)	On the lower rock walls of the inscribed rocks on the southern side of the West Peak of Jiuri Mountain
6	The inscription by Zhao Shigeng and others in winter's wind-praying ceremonies in the Song Dynasty	On the 21st day of lunar November of the 7th year of Chunyou Period (1247)	Zhao Shigeng (the Prefect and the Superintendent in charge of the Maritime Trade Office) from Kaifeng	On the lower rock walls of the inscribed rocks on the southern side of the West Peak of Jiuri Mountain
7	The inscription by Xie Zhi and others in winter's wind-praying ceremonies in the Song Dynasty	In lunar December of the 5th year of Baoyou Period (1257)	Zhao Shiyu (the official in charge of the Southern Clan Office) from Tianshui	On the upper cliffs on the southern side of the inscribed rocks at the eastern foot of the West Peak of Jiuri Mountain
8	The inscription by Fang Chengsun and others in summer's wind-praying ceremonies in the Song Dynasty	On the 28th day of lunar April of the 6th year of Baoyou Period (1258)	Zhao Shifan	On the northernmost cliffs of the inscribed rocks of the West Peak of Jiuri Mountain
9	The inscription by Zhao Xicha and others in winter's wind-praying ceremonies in the Song Dynasty	On the 10th day after the winter solstice in the 2nd year of Xianchun Period (1266)	Zhao Xicha (the Prefect and the Minister in charge of the Southern Clan Office) from Kaifeng, Zhao Chongdong from Wenzhou	On the southern cliffs of the eastern slope of the West Peak of Jiuri Mountain, where the inscription "Jiuri Mountain" was carved

宋代斗茶之风盛行，文人士大夫在九日山莲花峰留下众多题刻，记录当时茶事之盛。淳祐七年（1247），担任泉州知州兼提举市舶司事的赵师耕到九日山举行祈风仪式，并于西峰留下题刻："淳祐丁未仲冬二十有一日，古汴赵师耕以郡兼舶祈风遂游。"翌日，赵师耕来到莲花峰斗茶，留下了"斗茶而归，淳祐丁未仲冬二十有二日古汴赵师耕题"的摩崖石刻。

During the Song Dynasty, *Doucha* (tea competition) was prevalent, and literati and officials left many inscriptions on Lianhua Peak of Jiuri Mountain to record the prosperity of tea culture at that time. In 1247, Zhao Shigeng, the Prefect of Quanzhou and the Superintendent of the Maritime Trade Office, came to Jiuri Mountain to hold a wind-praying ceremony and left an inscription on the West Peak: "On the 21st day of lunar November of the 7th year of Chunyou Period (1247), Zhao Shigeng, the Prefect and the Superintendent of the Maritime Trade Office from Bianjing (today's Kaifeng), participated in a wind-praying ceremony here." The next day, Zhao Shigeng went to Lianhua Peak to participate in a *Doucha* competition and left a cliff inscription with: "Returning after the *Doucha* competition, on the 22nd day of lunar November of the 7th year of Chunyou Period, Zhao Shigeng from Bianjing inscribed these characters."

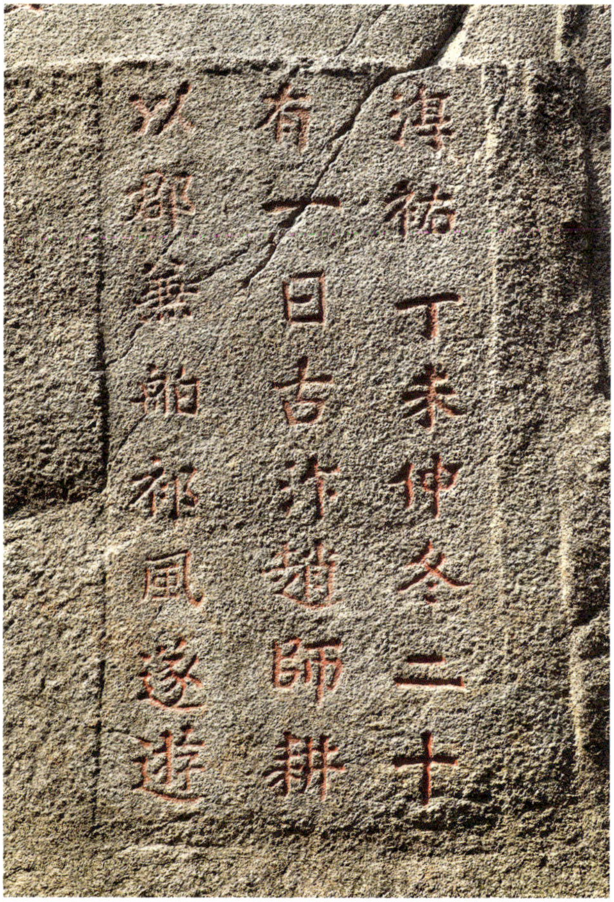

九日山西峰赵师耕题刻。（成冬冬 摄）
The inscription left by Zhao Shigeng on the West Peak of Jiuri Mountain. (Photo by Cheng Dongdong)

南宋绍兴二十三年（1153），赵氏宗室人员赵令衿任泉州知州，在安平桥落成后写有《东桥碑记》，今碑已佚。1928年《重修东桥碑记》载：“安海之有东桥，创自绍兴癸酉，成于太守赵公，事纪前碑，民歌德政。”

In 1153 of the Southern Song Dynasty, Zhao Lingjin, a member of the Zhao-surnamed imperial clan, became the Prefect of Quanzhou. Upon the completion of Anping Bridge, he wrote an inscription called *Inscription on the East Bridge*, which was lost. In 1928, the *Inscription on Repairing of the East Bridge* recorded: "There is an East Bridge in Anhai, which was begun to build in the year of Guiyou during Shaoxing Period and completed by the Prefect Zhao (Lingjin). The previous inscription was mentioned here to praise Zhao Lingjin's good governance."

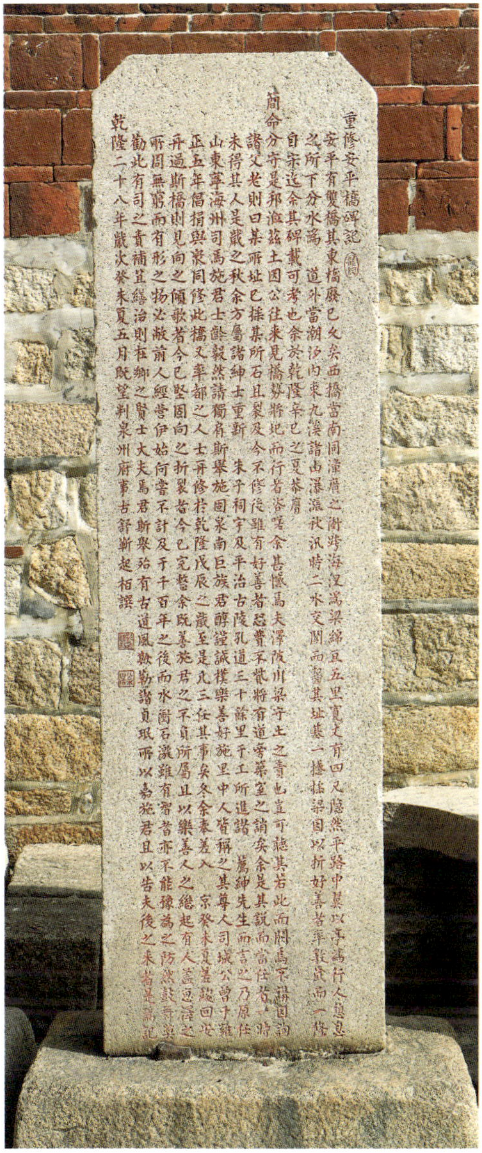

《重修东桥碑记》与安平桥。（成冬冬 摄）
The *Inscription on Repairing of the East Bridge* and Anping Bridge. (Photo by Cheng Dongdong)

赵必愿作为宗室人员，在淳熙中以华文阁直学士担任泉州知州，曾罢白土课及免差吏榷铁，旱灾时还开仓赈济灾民。咸淳元年（1265），南外宗人、泉州知州赵希侘主持修缮泉州府文庙大成殿。

在泉州海外交通史博物馆中，展示有一方南宋淳熙十三年（1186）铁制买地券。该买地券出土于泉州南安，由泉州南外宗人赵不劬为其母所置。买地券一般用砖 、铅板或石板刻文，此券则为铁铸阳文，反映了宋代的冶炼技术与铸铁工艺。

As a member of the imperial clan, Zhao Biyuan served as the governor of Quanzhou during 1174 and 1189 as an official of Huawen Academy. He abolished the land tax and exempted the labor duty of people in iron-producing regions. During times of drought, he also opened the granaries to provide relief to the affected residents.In 1265, Zhao Xicha, a member of the Southern Clan and governor of Quanzhou, presided over the renovation of Dacheng Hall of Confucian Temple in Quanzhou.

In Quanzhou Maritime Museum, there is an iron certificate of land purchase made in 1186 of the Southern Song Dynasty. Unearthed in Nan'an, Quanzhou, it was purchased by a member of the Southern Clan, Zhao Buqu, for his mother. Usually, land purchase certificates were inscribed on bricks, lead plates, or stone slabs, but this iron certificate was cut in relief, reflecting the smelting technology and iron-casting craftsmanship of the Song Dynasty.

南宋淳熙十三年（1186）铁制买地券。（成冬冬 摄）
The iron certificate of land purchase made in 1186 of the Southern Song Dynasty. (Photo by Cheng Dongdong)

南外宗室从中原地区带来先进生产工具及技术，促进泉州纺织技艺的提高，传播了中原的宫廷文化，发展了泉州本土曲艺文化及武术拳种，如“七子班”与梨园戏，五祖拳中的太祖拳等。此外，他们还推动了泉州本地社会经济、风俗文化的发展。

泉州南外宗正司遗址作为闽南地区首次科学发掘的具有独特修筑方式的宋元时期建筑遗迹，是目前进行考古发掘的唯一一处宋代宗正司遗址，遗存规格和丰富性充分说明了其在宋元时期的重要地位，进一步证明泉州在宋代以来海上贸易的重要作用。在考古遗址上建成的遗址公园，向世人展示南外宗正司的千年风华。

梨园戏《陈三五娘》。（吴刚强 摄）
Liyuan Opera *Chen San and Wu Niang*. (Photo by Wu Gangqiang)

Members of the Southern Clan brought advanced production tools and techniques from the Central Plains, which promoted the improvement of textile skills in Quanzhou and spread the court culture of the Central Plains. They also developed the local opera culture and martial arts, such as Liyuan Opera as well as Taizu Boxing of Wuzu Boxing (Five Ancestor Boxing). In addition, they also promoted the development of social economy and custom and culture in Quanzhou.

The site of Quanzhou Southern Clan Office, a relic originated from the Song and Yuan Dynasties with a unique construction method, was scientifically excavated for the first time in Southern Fujian. It is currently the only excavated site of the clan offices in the Song Dynasty. The scale and richness of the remaining relics fully show its importance during the Song and Yuan Dynasties, and further demonstrate Quanzhou's important role in maritime trade since the Song Dynasty. The heritage park built on the archaeological site will showcase the millennia splendor of the Southern Clan Office to the world.

泉州南少林寺僧人在学习五祖拳。（陈英杰 摄）
The monks in Quanzhou Southern Shaolin Temple are learning to play Wuzu Boxing. (Photo by Chen Yingjie)

海滨邹鲁，圣域津梁——泉州文庙与学宫

Quanzhou Confucian Temple and School: Sacred Bridge with Rich Culture

泉州的儒家文化

The Confucian Culture in Quanzhou

东南七省之冠的泉州府文庙

zhou Confucian Temple: the Largest among the Confucian Temples in Seven Southeastern Provinces in China

泉州书院与文化精英群体的崛起

Quanzhou's Academies and the Rise of the Cultural Elite Group

泉州府文庙牌坊。（田米 摄）
The memorial archway of Quanzhou Confucian Temple. (Photo by Tian Mi)

文庙是古代官方纪念和祭祀儒家思想创始人孔子的场所，作为兴学教化场所的学宫则是古代地方最高等级的教育机构。泉州府文庙及学宫作为泉州儒学的传播中心，是泉州包括政府官员和高级知识分子在内的泉州精英群体的象征。这些社会精英在推动和管理宋元海洋贸易中发挥了重要作用。

泉州府文庙和学宫鸟瞰图。（陈英杰 摄）
The aerial view of Quanzhou Confucian Temple and School. (Photo by Chen Yingjie)

Confucian Temples served as the official site for commemorating and worshipping Confucius, the founder of Confucianism. Confucian schools, places for promoting education and moral cultivation, represented the highest level of educational institutions in local areas in ancient time. As the dissemination center of Confucianism in Quanzhou, Quanzhou Confucian Temple and School symbolized the elite group, including government officials and senior intellectuals. These social elites played a significant role in promoting and managing the maritime trade during the Song and Yuan Dynasties.

泉州的儒家文化

自汉人南迁入闽以后，中原传统儒家文化也随之传入闽南。据史书记载，“永嘉之乱，衣冠南渡，始入闽者八族”，其中林、黄、陈、郑、詹、邱、何、胡八姓皆为中原大族。他们入闽后先在闽北建安（今建瓯）及闽东晋安（今福州）定居，而后逐渐扩散至闽中和闽南沿海地区，史称“衣冠南渡，八姓入闽”。这是中原地区人民第一次大规模南迁，也是北方汉人与闽人的第一次大融合。

伴随着宋代泉州海外贸易的兴盛，在地方官员兴学重教的倡导以及流寓于此的文人讲学推动下，泉州的文教事业得以不断发展。随着泉州地方科举的勃兴，温陵一郡科名鼎盛，理学得以传承并发扬光大。宋代的泉州科举取得了长足进步，其进士数量在中国东南沿海地区首屈一指，曾创下一榜四十名进士的纪录，造就了大批高等级人才。当时泉州的进士人数达到全国进士总数的三十分之一，为泉州赢得了“八闽形胜无双地，四海人文第一邦”的美誉。

The Confucian Culture in Quanzhou

Since the Han people moved southward to Fujian, the traditional Confucian culture of the Central Plains has also spread to Southern Fujian. According to historical records: "In the Disaster of Yongjia (311), the gentry who fled to the south were mainly from eight tribes." These tribes are surnamed Lin, Huang, Chen, Zheng, Zhan, Qiu, He and Hu, and they were big clans from the Central Plains. After entering Fujian, they first settled in Jian'an (Jian'ou nowadays) of northern Fujian and Jin'an (Fuzhou nowadays) in eastern Fujian, and then gradually spread to central and southern coastal areas of Fujian, known as "the gentry fled to the south, with eight tribes entering Fujian". This is the first large-scale southward migration from the Central Plains, and the first integration of the Han people from the north with those people in Fujian.

With the prosperity of Quanzhou's foreign trade during the Song Dynasty, through the advocacy of local officials prioritizing education and culture, and the promotion of scholars living there, Quanzhou's cultural and educational undertakings continued to develop. With its local imperial examinations flourishing, Quanzhou became renowned for its academic achievement, and Neo-Confucianism was able to be inherited and prosper. During the Song Dynasty, Quanzhou made great progress in imperial examinations, with the number of scholars (successful candidates in the highest imperial examinations) ranking among the top in southeastern coastal regions of China. The city nurtured numerous high-level talents and set a record of 40 scholars on a single examination list. At that time, the scholars in Quanzhou accounted for one thirtieth of the whole nation's, earning for Quanzhou the reputation "the most splendid and unmatched area among the eight prefectures of Fujian, and the most civilized prefecture across the whole country".

终宋一代，泉州可考知姓名的进士人数达到 1,418 位。这不仅位居福建各州府前列，且在全国也都占有一定地位。（成冬冬 摄）
During the Song Dynasty, a total of 1,418 were successful candidates in the highest imperial examinations and had their names recorded in Quanzhou. This achievement not only placed Quanzhou ahead of other prefectures in Fujian, but also established its prominent position in China. (Photo by Cheng Dongdong)

12 世纪的闽南精英阶层在政界和商界都享有广泛的机遇，为官者贯彻国家政令、主导地方政治；从商者积聚财富并建立宗族人脉关系网络。宋代泉州地方教育水平的提高与社会和城乡建设的发展表现出同步的特征，体现了社会精英对地方政治、经济、文化、技术发展的突出贡献。这些社会精英也是儒家、道家和佛家等主流意识形态的践行主体。

During the 12th century, the elite class in Southern Fujian enjoyed extensive opportunities in both politics and commerce. Government officials implemented national policies and led local politics, while business people accumulated wealth and established networks of familial relationships. The improvement of local education and the social and urban construction in Quanzhou during the Song Dynasty exhibits synchronous characteristics, highlighting the prominent contributions of social elites to local political, economic, cultural, and technological development. These social elites are also the main practitioners of mainstream ideologies of Confucianism, Taoism, and Buddhism.

泉州府文庙大成殿内的孔子塑像。（成冬冬 摄）
The statue of Confucius in Dacheng Hall of Quanzhou Confucian Temple. (Photo by Cheng Dongdong)

东南七省之冠的泉州府文庙

泉州被称为“海滨邹鲁”已有千年。泉州府文庙明伦堂前的“海滨邹鲁亭”中有一石碑，碑文为“接伊洛之渊源，开海滨之邹鲁”，可见泉州文风之盛。而在其中发挥重要作用的泉州府文庙与学宫始建于唐，形成于宋，完备于明清。泉州府文庙与学宫整体形制为“左学右庙”，即西侧是儒学祭祀建筑文庙，东侧是州级地方教育建筑学宫，由此也成为泉州传播传统儒家文化的中心。

泉州文庙最早建于唐开元末年，其址在衙城右侧，最初称“鲁司寇庙”，五代时改称“宣圣庙”。北宋太平兴国元年（976），知州乔维岳将其移建于崇阳门外三教铺，即今址。太平兴国七年（982），郡守孙逢吉即庙建学，自此泉州开始既有庙又有学，学宫正式形成。泉州府文庙主体格局形成于南宋绍兴七年（1137），此后代有修葺，文脉不坠。现存建筑为清乾隆二十六年（1761）重修时延续下来的格局，构成一个集宋、元、明、清四代建筑形式，较为完整的文庙建筑群。

Quanzhou Confucian Temple: the Largest among the Confucian Temples in Seven Southeastern Provinces in China

Quanzhou has enjoyed the name of a city rich in Confucian culture for over 1,000 years. A stone tablet standing in the Pavilion of *Haibin Zoulu* in front of Minglun Hall of Quanzhou Confucian Temple reads "Pass on the academic style of the Central Plains and build a coastal city rich in Confucian culture", deeply demonstrating the excellence of Quanzhou's education and culture. Quanzhou Confucian Temple and School, drivers in poetry and prose climate, were founded in the Tang Dynasty, took shape in the Song Dynasty, and reached their full completion during the Ming and Qing Dynasties. The overall layout of the complex is "school on the left and temple on the right", namely, the buildings dedicated to Confucian sacrifice in the west and the buildings serving the function of a prefecture-level institute of local education in the east. Thus the complex has been the center for the spread of traditional Confucian culture in Quanzhou.

Quanzhou Confucian Temple was first built in the late Kaiyuan Period (713—741) of the Tang Dynasty, located to the right of Yacheng (referring to the area where the local government administrative offices were located in ancient Chinese cities). It was initially called Lu Sikou Temple, and then renamed Xuansheng Temple during the Five Dynasties (907—960). In 976 of the Northern Song Dynasty, the Prefect Qiao Weiyue relocated it to *Sanjiao Pu* outside Chongyang Gate, the present site. In 982, the Prefect Sun Fengji built an academy in the temple. Since then, Quanzhou started to have both temple and academy, and the school officially took shape. The main layout of Quanzhou Confucian Temple took form in 1137 of the Southern Song Dynasty. Since then, it had undergone repairs and renovations, and the existing buildings are based on the renovation in 1761 of the Qing Dynasty, forming a relatively complete temple complex with architectural styles from the Song, Yuan, Ming and Qing Dynasties.

据不完全统计，泉州府文庙与学宫的大规模修建达 19 次之多。从建筑规模来看，泉州府文庙与学宫列中国东南七省文庙之冠，也是东南沿海乃至东南亚地区儒学文化传播的重要基地。

According to incomplete statistics, Quanzhou Confucian Temple and School have undergone major renovations and reconstructions as many as 19 times. It is the largest among the Confucian temples in the seven southeastern provinces in China, and is also an important base for the dissemination of Confucian culture in the southeast coast of China and even Southeast Asia.

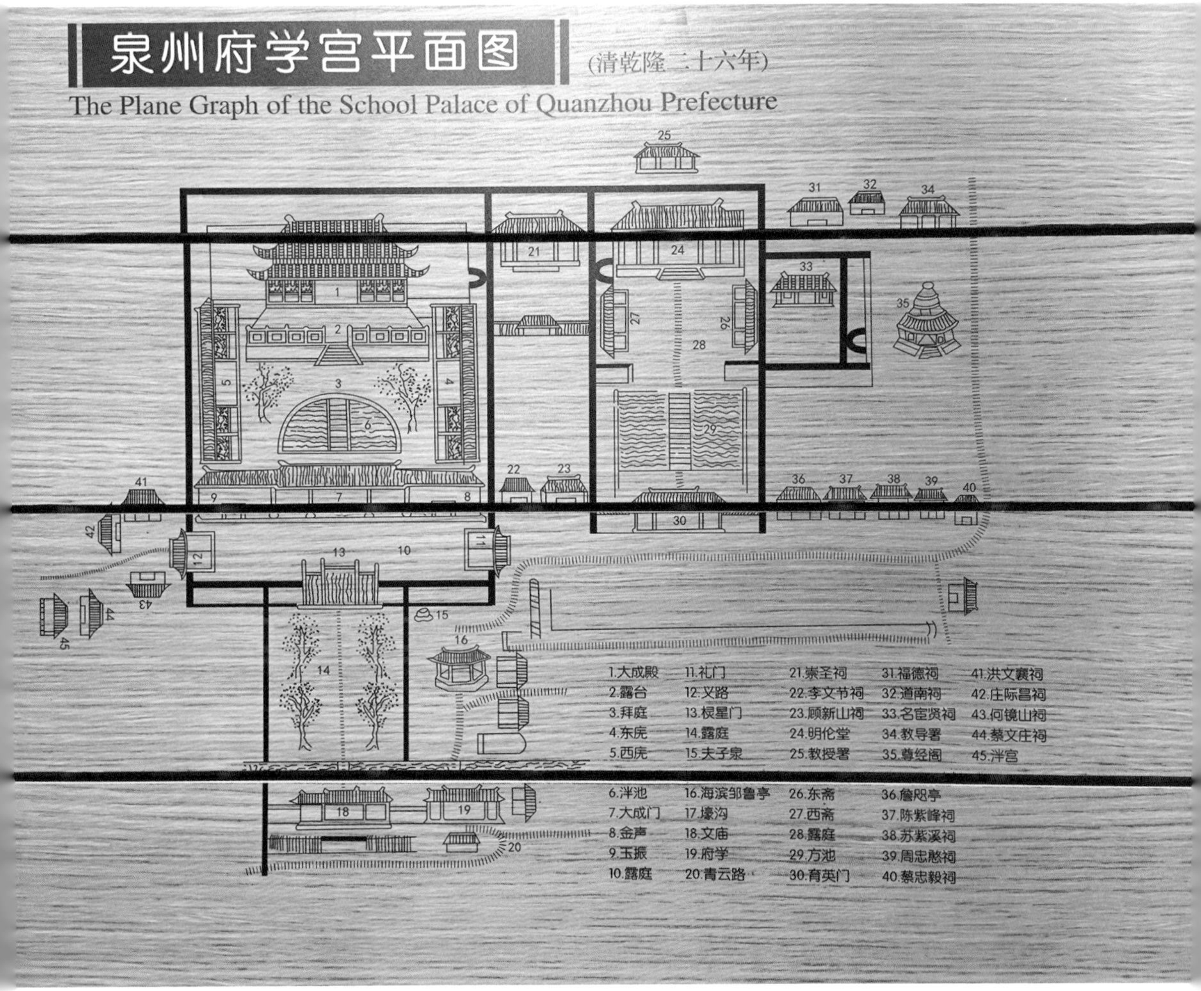

泉州府文庙与学宫平面图。（傅捷雄 摄）
The floor plan of Quanzhou Confucian Temple and School. (Photo by Fu Jiexiong)

泉州府文庙坐北朝南，由文庙和学宫两组建筑物组成，现占地面积 30,000 多平方米，建筑面积 5,000 多平方米。其总体布局由两条轴线组成：

文庙中轴线上由南而北依次为牌坊、洙泗桥、棂星门遗址、大成门、金声玉振门、泮池、泮桥、东西两庑、月台、大成殿；学宫中轴线上由南而北依次为照墙、育英门、学池、东西书斋、明伦堂等。此外，还附建有崇圣祠、名宦乡贤祠、泮宫门等各类单体建筑。

The building complex, facing southward with two axes, consists of the Confucian Temple and School, which cover over 30,000 square meters with a floor space of more than 5,000 square meters.

Proceeding from south to north along the axis of the west group of buildings which constitutes the Confucian Temple are the memorial archway, Zhusi Bridge, the remnants of Lingxing Gate, followed by Dacheng Gate, Jinsheng Gate, Yuzhen Gate, Panchi Pond and Pan Bridge, the east and west corridor rooms, the worship courtyard, and finally Dacheng Hall. Proceeding from south to north along the axis of the east group of buildings which constitutes the Confucian School are Spirit Screen, Yuying Gate, followed by the Study Pond and Study Bridge, east and west studies, and finally Minglun Hall. Besides, there are some single buildings, including Chongsheng Memorial Hall, memorial halls for famous officials and country worthies, and Pangong Gate.

洙泗桥。（李芸生 摄）
Zhusi Bridge. (Photo by Li Yunsheng)

文庙作为古代的礼制性建筑，其规格、样式严格按照传统儒家的礼仪精神与教育意图来构筑。文庙的入口为大成门，两侧为金声门、玉振门。孟子曰：“孔子之谓集大成。集大成也者，金声而玉振之也。”故以“大成”来表示孔子思想集古代先圣先贤之大成，金声、玉振则是赞颂孔子对文化的巨大贡献。

Confucian Temple, a ritual architecture, was constructed strictly in accordance with the traditional etiquette and educational intention of the ancient Confucian school. The entrance gate is Dacheng Gate, with Jinsheng Gate and Yuzhen Gate on both sides. Mencius once said: "Confucius is called the Master of Great Accomplishment. Everyone who deserves the title must be knowledgeable." Dacheng means great achievements, referring that Confucius had assembled all the great achievements from wise ancestral scholars. Jinsheng and Yuzhen (originally describing the resonance and harmony of music and later becoming a metaphor for a person's profound knowledge and exquisite talent) represent the respects paid to Confucius for his utmost contribution to Chinese culture.

大成门。（成冬冬 摄）
Dacheng Gate. (Photo by Cheng Dongdong)

泮池作为文庙建筑群的固定配置，是一种古老的建筑形制。泉州府文庙泮池开凿于南宋绍兴七年（1137），原为方形，明万历四十年（1612）改为半圆形。泮池的水与泉州的内河相连，可通潮汐，保证旱时不枯、涝时不溢，并兼具蓄水消防的功能。泮池之上的石桥被称为泮桥，建于元至正九年（1349），泮桥两侧护以栏杆。桥上有七十二条石板，隐喻孔子门下的七十二贤人，栏柱上雕刻的石象则象征太平景象。

Panchi Pond, a fixture on the building complex, is an old design. Panchi Pond was dug in 1137 of the Southern Song Dynasty. Originally square, it was changed to be semi-circular in 1612 of the Ming Dynasty. Panchi Pond connects to the inland rivers of Quanzhou, which enables the tides to circulate and prevents the water from drying up in drought or flooding in rain. Another critical function of the pond is as a water reserve in case of fire. The stone bridge over Panchi Pond, also known as Pan Bridge, was established in 1349 with railings on both sides. The 72 stone slabs, embedded on the bridge, symbolize the 72 well-known sages of Confucius. The stone statues of elephants on both ends of the bridge symbolize the harmonious society at that time.

泮池与泮桥、泮桥栏柱上的石象。（陈英杰 摄）

Panchi Pond, Pan Bridge and the stone statues of elephants on both ends of the bridge. (Photo by Chen Yingjie)

大成殿作为府文庙建筑群的核心，是祭祀孔子的中心场所。大成殿面阔七间，殿身由四十八根白圆石柱承托，重檐庑殿顶、黄色琉璃瓦、龙纹柱身、殿内通饰彩绘等显示出其非同寻常的建筑规格，反映了海洋贸易给泉州带来的经济和文化繁荣。

大成殿正中供奉着“大成至圣先师”孔子塑像，两旁配祀有颜回、孔伋、曾参、孟轲。殿内东西两侧还设有两龛，分别供奉闵子骞、仲弓、子贡、子路、子夏、有若、冉耕、宰予、冉求、子游、子张、朱熹十二贤哲的塑像。

现存大成殿的格局、石柱、木构梁架等建筑风格，仍保存有十二世纪的特征和历史信息。（成冬冬 摄）
The architectural style of the existing Dacheng Hall, including its layout, pillars, beams, and frames, still preserves the characteristics and historical information of the 12th century. (Photo by Cheng Dongdong)

Dacheng Hall, the central building of Confucian Temple complex, is the center for worshiping Confucius. It is seven *chien* (referring to bay) wide with its main body supported by forty-eight white marble pillars. It has double eave hip roof, yellow-glazed tiles, dragon pattern pillars and decorative paintings which are of extraordinary building standards of traditional Chinese architecture, representing the economic and cultural prosperity brought to Quanzhou by maritime trade in the Song and Yuan Dynasties.

In the centre of Dacheng Hall stands a statue of Confucius titled "The Sage and Master of the Great Accomplishments". On both sides are statues of attendant disciples including Yan Hui, Kong Ji, Zeng Sen and Meng Ke. On the east and west sides of the hall are two niches, enshrining statues of the Twelve Worthies including Min Ziqian, Zhonggong, Zigong, Zilu, Zixia, You Ruo, Ran Geng, Zai Yu, Ran Qiu, Ziyou, Zizhang and Zhu Xi.

两千多年来，儒家思想因符合统治需要受到历代帝王的大力推崇和提倡。在大成殿上方的梁枋上悬挂的匾额有清康熙皇帝御书“万世师表”、雍正皇帝御书“生民未有”、乾隆皇帝御书“与天地参”、嘉庆皇帝御书“圣集大成”、道光皇帝御书“圣协时中”、咸丰皇帝御书“德齐帱载”、同治皇帝御书“圣神天纵”、光绪皇帝御书“斯文在兹”、宣统皇帝御书“中和位育”和民国总统黎元洪的“道洽大同”等匾额，匾文内容极力赞颂孔子的高超品德以及他为中国古代教育做出的杰出贡献。

The past 2,000 years has seen the great promotion of Confucianism in all ages as it is in line with the ruling requirements. Above the beams and tiebeams of Dacheng Hall, there are several plaques inscribed by successive emperors from Kangxi to Xuantong in the Qing Dynasty and President Li Yuanhong of the Republic of China. Each plaque highly praises Confucius for his noblest moral character and his outstanding contributions to ancient Chinese education.

大成殿内景。（陈英杰 摄）
The interior view of Dacheng Hall. (Photo by Chen Yingjie)

大成殿内挂着多位帝王书写的牌匾。（刘宝生 摄）
The plaques written by several emperors in Dacheng Hall. (Photo by Liu Baosheng)

在金声玉振门后至大成殿前的东西两侧为两庑，东西各18开间，原为供奉孔子弟子七十二贤人及后世圣贤牌位，现辟为泉州市情和泉州府文庙展览的场地。

大成殿前的月台是古代文武官员举行祭孔仪式和献歌献舞的地方，古代祭孔时“八佾舞于庭”即在此举行。

On both sides of the path from Jinsheng Gate and Yuzhen Gate to Dacheng Hall, there are two wing rooms, each with 18 *chiens*. Originally, they were used to enshrine the tablets of the 72 disciples of Confucius and following saints and sages. Now they are used as an exhibition site for the overview of Quanzhou and Quanzhou Confucian Temple.

The platform in front of Dacheng Hall was designed for holding sacrificial rituals and music and dance performances in ancient times. When performing ceremonies to worship Confucius, *Bayi* Dance (eight rows of dancers in the courtyard), which can only be enjoyed by the emperor in the old times, is performed here.

泉州府文庙祭孔仪式。（闽人 供图）
Confucius-commemorating rituals at Quanzhou Confucian Temple. (Courtesy of Minren)

学宫所在的明伦堂于南宋绍兴七年（1137）创建，现存建筑为明正统年间重建。明伦堂面阔七间，进深五间，单檐硬山顶，穿斗式构架。堂内立 48 根粗大圆木柱，柱础为覆盆式素面，前廊立 8 根方石柱。明伦堂整体建筑规制在传统州府级中也是不多见的，现有泉州教育史话专题陈列。

Minglun Hall was first built in 1137 of the Southern Song Dynasty, and the existing building was rebuilt between 1436 and 1449 of the Ming Dynasty. Minglun Hall has a width of 7 *chiens* and a depth of 5 *chiens*. It has a single-eave gabled roof and is a column and tie construction. Inside the hall are 48 thick round wooden columns with plain bases in the shape of inverted basins. The front porch has 8 square stone columns. The overall architectural style of the hall is rare among traditional prefectural-level schools, and it now houses an exhibition on the education history of Quanzhou.

明伦堂作为官方举办的学校，是古代泉州的最高学府。（成冬冬 摄）
Served as the official school, Minglun Hall was the education institution of the highest level in ancient Quanzhou. (Photo by Cheng Dongdong)

明伦堂前东西两侧有书斋，在露庭前则有学池与学桥，从其上走过寓意青云直上、平步青云；其入口处的大门称为育英门，意为培育英才的地方。

学池和学桥。（傅捷雄 摄）
School Pond and School Bridge. (Photo by Fu Jiexiong)

On the east and west sides in front of Minglun Hall are classrooms and in front of the worshiping courtyard are School Pond and School Bridge, which symbolize the ascent to great success. Yuying Gate serves as the main entrance to Minglun Hall. Yuying, literally in Chinese means to cultivate elites.

在泉州府文庙的西南侧近中山路建有一座泮宫门，又称圣贤门。泮宫门坐西朝东，其始建于 12 世纪，1914 年改为水泥仿木建筑，是泉州最早的水泥建筑。

泉州府文庙与学宫周边曾建有奉祀政绩突出的地方官和本地出身的著名官员与地方士绅、学者等社会名流的名宦乡贤祠，现则仅存崇圣祠、蔡清祠、李文节祠和庄际昌状元祠。

崇圣祠又称“启圣祠”，位于大成殿与明伦堂之间，为三进五开间硬山式建筑，是祭祀孔子五代先祖之所。

蔡清祠又称“蔡文庄公祠”，位于文庙广场西侧。蔡清祠为三进五开间硬山式建筑，崇祀明代著名理学家蔡清，为泉州府文庙附建的第一座乡贤专祠，现作为《泉州文库》整理出版委员会办公场所。

李文节祠位于金声门东侧，为两进三开间双边护硬山式建筑，奉祀明代东阁大学士李廷机。

庄际昌状元祠为三进三开间硬山式建筑，祀明代状元、宫詹庄际昌，现辟为“百姓书屋”。

泮宫门开创了西式建筑材料与中国传统木构建筑工艺结合的先河。（成冬冬 摄）

Pangong Archway represents the first application of western construction material to traditional Chinese wooden architecture. (Photo by Cheng Dongdong)

Sitting on the southwest side of Quanzhou Confucian Temple and facing Zhongshan Road, Pangong Archway, is also known as the Gate of Holy Sages. It was first built in the 12th century, facing east. Pangong Archway, the earliest building made of cement in Quanzhou, was restored in the traditional Chinese timber-framed style in 1914.

Quanzhou Confucian Temple and School were surrounded by the shrines dedicated to outstanding local officials, famous officials born in Quanzhou and local gentry, and prominent members of the intellectual community, honoring the achievements of these individuals and their contributions to the society. Today, only Chongsheng Memorial Hall, Caiqing Memorial Hall, Li Wenjie Memorial Hall, and Zhuang Jichang Memorial Hall remain.

Chongsheng Memorial Hall, also known as Qisheng Memorial Hall, is situated between Dacheng Hall and Minglun Hall. It is a three-quadrangle, five-*chien*, gabbled-roof building used for the worship of Confucius, Confucius' ancestors of five generations.

Caiqing Memorial Hall, also called Cai Wenzhuang Memorial Hall, is located in the west of Confucian Temple. It is a gabbled-roof architecture of three-quadrangle and five-*chien* style. In memory of the famous Neo-Confucianist Caiqing in the Ming Dynasty, it is the first memorial hall for renowned intellectuals in the compound of Quanzhou Confucian Temple. It is now used as the editorial office for compiling and publishing ancient precious documentation and literature of Quanzhou.

Wedged by bilateral guardhouses, Li Wenjie Memorial Hall is located on the east side of Jinsheng Gate, with a gabbled-roof architecture of two-quadrangle and three-*chien* style. It is dedicated to Li Tingji, a grand secretariat of the Ming Dynasty.

Zhuang Jichang Memorial Hall is a three-quadrangle, three-*chien*, gabbled-roof architecture that worships Zhuang Jichang, a top scholar and top assistant of the crown prince in the Ming Dynasty. It is now used as the People's Library.

李文节祠现为泉州南音传习所，人们可以在晚上到此欣赏南音雅乐演出。（成冬冬 摄）
Li Wenjie Memorial Hall is now used as the Nanyin Inheritance Center, where people could enjoy Nanyin here at night. (Photo by Cheng Dongdong)

洙泗桥位于文庙广场东南隅，横跨于八卦沟上。洙泗桥始建于明嘉靖四年（1525），其旁竖花岗岩石碑，上镌“洙泗桥”三个大字，落款为“嘉靖乙酉冬立石”。

夫子泉井在文庙广场东北隅，为南宋隆兴年间教授黄启宗于此掘得清泉。乾道年间，王十朋曾写诗赞颂。后因建露台人们将井填塞。明嘉靖三十三年（1554），教授唐尧宾重浚夫子泉于今址，上盖以石井圈，旁立石碑。

每年9月28日，泉州府文庙都会以最高规格“释奠礼”来祭祀孔子。每年的春节、中秋节等中华民族传统节日里，这里也会举行成年礼、拜师礼、毕业礼等活动，传统儒家文化在泉州得到很好的传承与延续。

泉州府文庙与学宫不仅是世遗之城泉州具有代表性的文化坐标，同时也展示了泉州绵延不绝的文化命脉。

夫子泉井旁石碑中刻“夫子泉”，左刻“宋王梅溪有诗”，右刻“嘉靖甲寅立石”。（成冬冬 摄）

On the stone tablet beside Fuzi (Confucius) Well, were engraved with “Fuzi Well” in the center, “Poem by Wang Meixi” on the left, and “Erected in the 33rd Year of Jiajing Period (1554)” on the right. (Photo by Cheng Dongdong)

Zhusi Bridge is located at the southeast corner of the Temple Square, spanning over the Bagua Ditch. The bridge was first built in 1525 of the Ming Dynasty. By the bridge stands a granite stele engraved with the characters "Zhusi Bridge" and the inscription "Erected in the winter of Yiyou Year of Jiajing Period (1525)".

Between 1163 and 1164 of the Southern Song Dynasty, Professor Huang Qizong excavated a clear spring at the northeast corner of the Temple Square, which is now the location of Fuzi Well. Between 1165 and 1173, the Prefect Wang Shipeng wrote poems to praise it. In order to build the patio, people filled in the well later. In 1554 of the Ming Dynasty, Professor Tang Yaobin re-excavated Fuzi Well at its current location, and covered it with a stone well circle and erected a stone tablet beside it.

On September 28, the birthday of Confucius, Quanzhou Confucian Temple will hold the highest standard ritual *Shidianli* to pay tribute to Confucius every year. On traditional festivals such as the Spring Festival, the Mid-autumn Festival, a variety of ceremonies such as the rite of passage ceremonies, teachers veneration ceremonies, and graduation activities are held in the temple for better sustaining and inheriting Confucianism.

Quanzhou Confucian Temple and School not only represent a typical cultural coordinate as a world heritage site, but also indicate the continuation of Quanzhou's culture.

参加泉州府文庙祭拜孔子活动后的孩子们展示他们领到的红蛋。（陈英杰 摄）

The children are showing their red-dyed eggs indicating edifying wisdom after they participate in the activity of worshiping Confucius in Quanzhou Confucian Temple. (Photo by Chen Yingjie)

泉州书院与文化精英群体的崛起

入宋以后，随着闽南经济的开发，尤其是南宋政治中心移跸杭州，泉州也得到较快发展。朱熹、真德秀、王十朋等硕儒先后于泉州讲学、任官，对泉州地方文化发展产生重要影响。彼时的泉州，官私之学并重，书院风行，人文荟萃，其中石井书院、泉山书院、小山丛竹书院与欧阳书院并称为泉州“四大书院”。

泉州宋代书院一览表

书院名称	院 址	创建时间	创建纪要
岩峰书院	永春达埔镇	绍兴十一年（1141）	名士陈知柔建
燕南书院	金门金城镇	绍兴二十三年（1153）	朱熹建
小山丛竹书院	州治城隍庙旁	绍兴二十三年至二十六年（1153—1156）	朱熹在原书斋基础上建
九日山书院	南安丰州镇		朱熹与傅自得建
文公书院	同安县城	嘉定年间（1208—1224）	知县毛君建
石井书院	晋江安海镇	嘉定四年（1211）	朱熹之子朱在主持修建
龙山书院	惠安螺山	嘉熙二年（1238）	知县郑子清建
科山书院	惠安科山	嘉熙二年（1238）	知县郑子清建
清源书院	州治袭魁坊	淳祐六年（1246）	知宗正事赵希衮建
泉山书院	州治行春门外	咸淳三年（1267）	知州赵宗正建，祀朱熹

Quanzhou's Academies and the Rise of the Cultural Elite Group

With the economic development in Southern Fujian in the Song Dynasty, especially after the shift of political center of the Southern Song Dynasty to Hangzhou, Quanzhou experienced rapid growth. Great efforts had been made for the development of local culture in Quanzhou, as seen in plenty of scholars, like Zhu Xi, Zhen Dexiu and Wang Shipeng, who gave lectures or took office here. Since equal importance was given to official schools and private schools, a galaxy of advanced culture and talents emerged and many academies flourished, among which Shijing Academy, Quanshan Academy, Xiaoshan Congzhu Academy and Ouyang Academy are collectively known as the "Four Great Academies of Quanzhou".

Table of Quanzhou's Academies in the Song Dynasty

Name	Location	Founding Time	Notes
Yanfeng Academy	Dapu Town, Yongchun County	1141	Built by Chen Zhirou, a local celebrity
Yannan Academy	Jincheng Town, Jinmen County	1153	Built by Zhu Xi
Xiaoshan Congzhu Academy	Near Town God's Temple, downtown Quanzhou	1153—1156	Built by Zhu Xi based on the original study
Jiurishan Academy	Fengzhou Town, Nan'an City		Built by Zhu Xi and Fu Zide
Wengong Academy	Tongan County	1208—1224	Built by County Magistrate Mao Jun
Shijing Academy	Anhai Town, Jinjiang City	1211	Built by Zhu Zai (Zhu Xi's son)
Longshan Academy	Luoshan, Hui'an County	1238	Built by County Magistrate Zheng Ziqing
Keshan Academy	Keshan, Hui'an County	1238	Built by County Magistrate Zheng Ziqing
Qingyuan Academy	Xikui Lane, downtown Quanzhou	1246	Built by Zhao Xigun, the Minister of the Southern Clan Office
Quanshan Academy	Outside Xingchun Gate, Quanzhou City	1267	Built by the Prefect Zhao Zongzheng in memory of Zhu Xi

石井书院，为泉州知州邹应龙于嘉定四年（1211）应地方士民之请，特命通判朱在（朱熹之子）于晋江安海主持修建。书院按州县学宫规制建造，并祀朱松、朱熹二先生像于尊德堂，以纪念朱熹父子讲学安海与“过化”之德。后世“慕朱先生之风”，屡有修葺。石井书院作为晋江最早创建且保存至今的书院，被列为泉州古代“四大书院”之首。

泉山书院，为泉州知州赵宗正于南宋咸淳三年（1267）在城东行春门外迁天宁寺所建。书院奉祀朱熹，并延聘名儒讲学，名噪一时。明初书院为晋江县学所占，正德十年（1515）移建于今东街蔡巷内，祠学分置。清乾隆七年（1742）知府王廷诤捐俸重修，建启贤祠以祀朱熹之父朱松，旁建敬业堂及学舍，并更名为“温陵书院”。

石井书院的前身为朱熹父亲朱松所建“鳌头精舍”。（成冬冬 摄）
Shijing Academy was originally Aotou Jingshe, a lecture hall, built by Zhu Song, Zhu Xi's father. (Photo by Cheng Dongdong)

In 1211, at the request of local gentry and commoners, Shijing Academy was established by Quanzhou Prefect Zou Yinglong and entrusted to Vice-Prefect of the Prefecture Zhu Zai (Zhu Xi's son) for construction and supervision in Anhai Town, Jinjiang. The academy was built according to the rules and regulations of county schools and academies, and the statues of the two masters, Zhu Song and Zhu Xi, were enshrined in Zunde Hall to commemorate the teaching of Zhu Xi and his father in Anhai and their moral influence. In later generations, many renovations were carried out due to the admiration of the moral principles of Zhu Xi. Shijing Academy, as the earliest and well-preserved academy in Jinjiang, is regarded as head of the "Four Great Academies of Quanzhou".

Replacing Tianning Temple, Quanshan Academy was built by Zhao Zongzheng, the Prefect of Quanzhou in 1267 of the Southern Song Dynasty outside Xingchun Gate to the east of the city. The academy worshipped Zhu Xi and invited famous scholars to lecture, making it a hit. In the early Ming Dynasty, the academy was used as Jinjiang County School. In 1515, it was moved into Cai Lane in East Street, with the memorial hall and school separated. In 1742 of the Qing Dynasty, the Prefect Wang Tingzheng donated his salary to repair the academy and established Qixian Memorial Hall to worship Zhu Song (Zhu Xi's father), with Jingye Hall and academic buildings close to the memorial hall. At the same time, it was renamed "Wenling Academy".

温陵书院碑记。（成冬冬 摄）
The tablet of Wenling Academy. (Photo by Cheng Dongdong)

小山丛竹书院原为资寿寺。南宋绍兴年间朱熹为同安主簿，以此处为郡城龙首之脉，曾种竹建亭讲学于此。《八闽通志》曾记："小山丛竹亭，在资寿寺内。宋绍兴间，朱熹为同安主簿，尝讲学于此。因书'小山丛竹'四字遗其僧。元至正间，僧泽润建亭，取以为名。"明李光缙亦云："朱文公为同安主簿，每抵郡城，必登小山，称其山川之美，为郡治龙首之脉。徘徊数日而后去，自书曰'小山丛竹'。"书院旁有纪念欧阳詹的"不二堂"，朱熹题有"事业经邦，闽海贤才开气运；文章华国，温陵甲第破天荒"联句。1925 年，小山丛竹辟为温陵养老院。1942 年，弘一法师圆寂于温陵养老院"晚晴室"。小山丛竹作为泉州文脉的重要发源地之一，被列为"泉州旧八景"之首。

欧阳书院，又称清源欧阳书室，旧址在清源山五台峰右侧之虎岩。欧阳书院原为唐代泉州名士欧阳詹及林蕴、林藻兄弟读书之所，因在城外，又有"刺桐城外读书台"之雅称。明成化十八年(1482)，张庸等人感念欧阳詹对泉州文教的影响，捐集资金倡修。嘉靖八年(1529)，欧阳詹的裔孙欧阳深及其子欧阳模捐赀拓地鼎新，书院的规制更为完备，有祠堂、讲堂、斋舍等。书院建成后，李开芳书"高山仰止"并刻于虎岩前；学者常聚集于此讲学研习，午夜书声可以相闻。

小山丛竹书院所在地曾被朱熹称为郡治龙首之脉。(成冬冬 摄)
Zhu Xi regarded Xiaoshan Congzhu Academy as an auspicious site. (Photo by Cheng Dongdong)

Xiaoshan Congzhu Academy was originally known as Zishou Temple. During 1131 and 1162 of the Southern Song Dynasty, Zhu Xi, who served as a clerk officer in Tong'an, regarded this place as the propitious omen of Quanzhou and thus planted bamboos, built a pavilion and taught here. *General Gazetteer of Fujian* once recorded, "Xiaoshan Congzhu Pavilion is located within Zishou Temple. During 1131 and 1162 of the Song Dynasty, Zhu Xi lectured here when he was a clerk officer in Tong'an. He wrote the Chinese calligraphy '小山丛竹 (Xiaoshan Congzhu)', meaning hills with bamboos, and presented them to a monk. During 1341—1368 of the Yuan Dynasty, the monk Zerun built the pavilion and named it accordingly." Li Guangjin of the Ming Dynasty also said, "Zhu Xi was the clerk officer in Tong'an and whenever he arrived at Quanzhou City, he would climb Xiaoshan Hill and praise it for the embodiment of the beauty of the mountains and rivers, calling it the auspicious sign of Quanzhou. Staying for several days, he left and wrote down 'Xiaoshan Congzhu'". Beside the academy is Bu'er Hall in memory of Ouyang Zhan, a famous poet from Quanzhou in the Tang Dynasty. Zhu Xi inscribed the couplet: "With a career to serve the country, Fujian has talented people to bring fortune; With writings to glorify the country, Wenling's top scholars break new ground." In 1925, the academy was transformed into Wenling Retirement Home. In 1942, Master Hongyi passed away in Wanqing Room here. As one of the important sources of Quanzhou's culture and literature, Xiaoshan Congzhu Academy is listed as the first of the "Eight Old Views of Quanzhou".

The former site of Ouyang Academy, or Qingyuan Ouyang Study, was located on the right side of the Tiger Rock, which was adjacent to the Wutai Peak of Qingyuan Mountain. Ouyang Academy was originally a place for Ouyang Zhan and the brothers Lin Yun and Lin Zao, the literati in the Tang Dynasty, to study in Quanzhou. As it was outside the city, it was also known as the "Reading Pavilion Outside Zayton City". In 1482 of the Ming Dynasty, Zhang Yong, and others, in memory of Ouyang Zhan for his influence on Quanzhou's culture and education, donated funds to renovate the academy. In 1529, Ouyang Zhan's descendant Ouyang Shen and his son Ouyang Mo donated money to expand the academy and improve the scale and design with memorial hall, lecture hall, dormitories, and other facilities. After the completion of the academy, Li Kaifang wrote the phrase "Gaoshan Yangzhi" (literally, "looking up to the high Mountain", metaphorically, "holding someone in the highest esteem") and had it engraved in front of the Tiger Rock. Scholars often gathered here to deliver lectures and pursue their studies, with their sound of reading audible even in the dead of night.

自宋元以来，在硕儒名宦的影响带动下，泉州本土文人整体水平也不断提升，涌现出如曾公亮、苏颂、梁克家、卢琦、蔡清、李贽、李光地等代表性人物。

曾公亮（999—1078），字明仲，号乐正，晋江人，北宋天圣二年（1024）登进士第，历仕仁宗、英宗、神宗三朝，累迁知制诰、史馆修撰、参知政事、同中书门下平章事、集贤殿大学士，其所编撰的《武经总要》为中国历史上第一部记述军事知识的总集，书中第一次完整记录了火药的配方与制造流程。曾公亮及其后世子孙曾孝宽、曾憕、曾从龙先后拜相，故有“一门四相”之美誉。

苏颂（1020—1101），字子容，同安人，北宋庆历二年（1042）登进士第，历任刑部尚书、吏部尚书、尚书右丞，元祐七年（1092）拜相，执政时务使百官守法遵职，不立党援，以礼自持。苏颂于经史及算法、本草等学皆有涉猎，是北宋杰出的天文机械制造家、药物学家，有《苏魏公文集》《新仪象法要》《本草图经》等作品传世。

苏颂与韩公廉合作制造的水运仪象台，是集浑仪、浑象和计时装置为一体的天文台，反映了宋代机械设计的高超水平。（闽人 供图）

The astronomical clock-tower invented by Su Song and Han Gonglian was a remarkable feat of mechanical design in the Song Dynasty, which integrated the functions of a celestial globe, an armillary sphere, and a timing device. (Courtesy of Minren)

Since the Song and Yuan Dynasties, with the influence of accomplished scholars and influential officials, Quanzhou has witnessed an increase of local literati, such as Zeng Gongliang, Su Song, Liang Kejia, Lu Qi, Cai Qing, Li Zhi, Li Guangdi, and other representative figures.

Zeng Gongliang (999—1078), known by his courtesy name Mingzhong and also referred to as Lezheng in his literary works, was born in Jinjiang, Quanzhou. In 1024, he passed the highest imperial examination and became one of the distinguished scholars. During the reigns of Emperors Renzong, Yingzong, and Shenzong, he got promotion multiple times and held various important positions such as Secretariat Drafter, Historica Archivist, Assistant Administrator, Joint Manager of Affairs with the Secretariat-Chancellery, and Grand Secretariat of Jixian Hall. He compiled *Complete Essentials for the Military Classics*, which is the first Chinese military compendium in history, recording the formula and process of manufacturing gunpowder. Zeng Gongliang and his descendants Zeng Xiaokuan, Zeng Zao, Zeng Conglong successively served as prime ministers. This impressive feat has earned them the reputation "four prime ministers from one family".

Su Song (1020—1101), known by his courtesy name Zirong, was born in Tongan, Quanzhou (Tongan District, Xiamen nowadays). He passed the highest imperial examination and became one of the distinguished scholars in 1042. He served successively as the Administrator of Ministry of Justice, Administrator of Ministry of Personnel, Prime Minister, and was promoted as the Chancellor in 1092. During his term in office, he upheld proper conduct and all officials followed the law and carried out their duties without resorting to partisan politics. As an expert in astronomical machinery manufacturing and pharmacology, he had a broad range of knowledge in various fields covering history, literature, mathematics, astronomy, mechanics, and herbal. Also, he left a legacy of works such as *The Collected Writings of Su Weigong*, *Essential Techniques of Astronomy and Calendrical Science*, and *Illustrated Pharmacopoeia*.

梁克家（1127—1187），字叔子，晋江人，自幼聪敏，勤奋自励，书过目成诵。南宋绍兴三十年（1160）梁克家廷试第一，高中状元，累官至端明殿学士、佥书枢密院事、参知政事，拜右丞相，封仪国公。

卢琦（1306—1362），字希韩，号奎峰、立斋，惠安人。元至正二年（1342）中进士，曾任永春、德化县尹，福建盐科提举，所至颇有政声。卢琦文品诗名卓著，备受世人推崇，与陈旅、林以顺、林泉生同被誉为"元末闽中文学四大名士"，有《奎峰集》二卷传世。后人赞其："元诗三十大家选，公诗澹远，意境绝高，出三十大家上，盖韦、孟之诗也。"卢琦对明代八闽诗坛有较大影响，明"闽中十才子"的诗受他影响颇巨。

蔡清（1453—1509），字介夫，号虚斋，泉州人。明成化二十年（1484）蔡清中进士，累官礼部祠祭司主事、吏部稽勋司主事、礼部祠祭司员外郎、南京文选司郎中、江西提学副使、南京国子监祭酒，有《四书蒙引》《虚斋文集》等传世。作为著名理学家，其学说主张"静""虚"，有"八闽文献之宗"之美誉，尤其在易学自成一家，并形成"清源学派"，志书称"至今天下言《易》者，皆推晋江；成弘间士大夫谈理学，惟蔡清尤为精诣"。

图为梁克家墓。梁克家著有《淳熙三山志》《中兴会要》等，其文"浑厚明白，自成一家，辞命尤温雅，多行于世"。（成冬冬 摄）

This is Liang Kejia's tomb. Liang Kejia, the author of such works as *Annals of Fuzhou in Chunxi Period* and *Essentials of the Revival in the Southern Song Dynasty*, is renowned for his writing style that is profound and clear, distinctive, and particularly elegant in its diction, which has been widely circulated. (Photo by Cheng Dongdong)

Liang Kejia (1127—1187), known by his courtesy name Shuzi, was born in Jinjiang, Quanzhou. With his intelligence, diligence, and a very good visual memory, he won the first place in the highest imperial examination in 1160. He was successively appointed as the secretary of Duanming Palace, assistant of the Chief Military Commission, Assistant Administrator, promoted to the Chancellor and bestowed the title of Duke Yi.

Lu Qi (1306—1362), known by his courtesy name Xihan, and also referred to as Kuifeng and Lizhai in his literary works, was born in Hui'an, Quanzhou. In 1342 of the Yuan Dynasty, Lu was one of the nominees who passed the highest imperial examination. He served as the magistrate of Yongchun and Dehua counties, and the tax supervisor of Fujian Salt Office. He gained a commendable reputation for his governance wherever he held office. Lu is well known for his poetry and prose, and is praised as one of the "Four Great Literati of Fujian at the End of the Yuan Dynasty" alongside Chen Lyu, Lin Yishun, and Lin Quansheng. His two-volume collection of poems, *Kuifeng Essay Collection*, has been passed down through the ages. Later generations once praised him: "Lu's poetry, sublime and far-reaching, is one of the thirty greatest works of Yuan poetry with extraordinary scenes and ideas, and it can be ranked alongside Wei Yingwu and Meng Haoran's poetry." Lu Qi had a significant influence on Fujian poets in the Ming Dynasty, especially on the "Ten Talented Poets of Fujian in the Ming Dynasty".

Cai Qing (1453—1509), known by his courtesy name Jiefu and also referred to as Xuzhai in his literary works, was born in Quanzhou. Cai Qing was one of the nominees who passed the highest imperial examination in 1484. He served as Director of Sacrifices and Ceremonies Department of the Ministry of Rites, Department of Checking and Reviewing Meritorious Services in the Ministry of Personnel, the Vice Minister of the Department of Sacrifices and Ceremonies in the Ministry of Rites, the Rectifier of the Directorate of Literary Department of the Ministry of Rites in Nanjing, the Assistant Commissioner of Education in Jiangxi, and the Vice President of the Imperial Academy in Nanjing. He composed such classics as *Beginnings of the Four Books* and *Xuzhai Collected Works*. As a famous Neo-Confucian scholar, he advocated "stillness" and "emptiness", earning him the title "The Patriarch of Fujian Literature". In the study of *The Book of Changes*, he established his own school of thought, known as the "Qingyuan School". The local annals once commented, "It is said that till today, all those who speak of *The Book of Changes* cite Jinjiang; during the Chenghua and Hongzhi era (1465—1505), literati discussing Neo-Confucianism regarded Cai Qing as possessor of the greatest insight."

蔡清卒后被追谥“文庄”，从祀泉州文庙。（成冬冬 摄）
Cai Qing was posthumously honored with the title "Wenzhuang" and enshrined in Quanzhou Confucian Temple. (Photo by Cheng Dongdong)

李贽（1527—1602），原名载贽，字宏甫，号卓吾，别号温陵居士，泉州人，为明代著名思想家、文学家。李贽反对理学空谈，倡导功利价值，主张“革故鼎新”和个性解放，反对思想禁锢，提出了“至道无为、至治无声、至教无言”的政治理想。李廷机在《祭李卓吾文》中赞道：“心胸廓八肱，识见洞千古。孑然置一身于太虚中，不染一尘，不碍一物，清净无欲，先生有焉。盖吾乡士大夫未有如先生者，即海内如先生者亦少矣。”泉州鲤城区万寿路有李贽故居，为其青少年时代居住的地方，故居内有李贽塑像及生平展览，以供世人瞻仰。

李贽一生著述颇丰，其重要著作有《焚书》《续焚书》《藏书》《续藏书》《史纲评要》等。（成冬冬 摄）
Li Zhi is a prolific thinker and litterateur with magnum opus like *Of Burning Books*, *Continuation of Burning Books*, *Of Collecting Books*, *Continuation of Collecting Books*, and *A History of China with Commentaries*. (Photo by Cheng Dongdong)

Li Zhi (1527—1602), born Li Zaizhi, Hongfu by courtesy name and often known by his pseudonym Zhuowu or Wenling Householder, was a well-known philosopher and litterateur from Quanzhou in the Ming Dynasty. In contrast to the prevailing Neo-Confucian discourse, Li Zhi preached utilitarianism, and advocated reform and innovation and emancipation of individuality. He opposed ideological imprisonment and proposed a political ideal of " 'non-action' is the ultimate way, 'silence' the ultimate governance, and 'wordlessness' the ultimate teaching". Li Tingji, a famous official of the late Ming Dynasty, praised him in the *Sacrifice to Li Zhuowu*: "His mind is spacious and his knowledge is profound and far-reaching. He lives alone in the void, untainted by dust or unyoked. He is pure and desireless. There have been few gentlemen in my hometown or even in the whole country like him." Li Zhi's former residence in Wanshou Road, Licheng District is the place where he lived in his youth. In it are a statue of Li Zhi and the exhibition of his biography for people to pay a visit.

李光地（1642—1718），字晋卿，号厚庵，别号榕村，安溪人，清初理学名臣。李光地于康熙九年（1670）中进士，选庶吉士，此后历任翰林院编修、翰林学士、兵部右侍郎、工部左侍郎、顺天督学、直隶巡抚，累官至文渊阁大学士兼吏部尚书，有《朱子礼纂》《性理精义》《榕村文集》等传世。李光地在政治上清廉勤政，公忠体国，秉持大义，不拘小节，其曾协助平定三藩之乱，力主收复台湾维护国家统一，同时还着力于治理河务、免除赋税等。

李光地故居位于安溪县湖头镇中山街，厅前悬挂“夹辅高风”匾额，为康熙帝所赐。湖头镇湖四村的俊民中学边有“榕村书屋”，即贤良祠，厅堂内外环墙嵌大理石，镌刻有康熙御书《太极图说》《巡子牙河建坝诗》等诗文。祠右有石构碑亭，立有雍正《谕祭文》碑，赞扬李光地为“一代之完人”。

李光地位于安溪湖头镇的故居。（刘伯怡 摄）
Li Guangdi's former residence, located in Hutou Town, Anxi County. (Photo by Liu Boyi)

Li Guangdi (1642—1718), known by his courtesy name Jinqing, and also referred to as Houan and Rongcun in his literary works, was a prominent Chinese Neo-Confucianist court official during the early Qing Dynasty. He hailed from Anxi County. In 1670, he was one of the nominees who passed the highest imperial examination and was selected to Hanlin Academy for learning. Throughout his life, Li held various court positions, including the editor and secretary of the Imperial Academy, the assistant minister of the Ministry of Wars, Education Inspector of Shuntian Prefecture, grand coordinator, and Governor of the Capital and rose to grand secretary of the Imperial Library and Concurrent Administrator of the Ministry of Personnel. Li wrote or edited a number of classics, including the *Complete Works of Zhu Xi*, the *Essential Ideas of Nature and Principle* and the *Collected Works of Rongcun*. Li is an upright and diligent official who is loyal to the country and upholds the principles of justice. He did not get bogged down in trivial matters. With his assistance in defeating Wu Sangui, Geng Jingzhong and Shang Kexi, three feudatories against the Qing Dynasty, Emperor Kangxi eventually quelled the revolt. Later in life, he strongly advocated the recovery of Taiwan to uphold national unity. Additionally, he focused on the management of river affairs and the reduction of taxes.

Li Guangdi's former residence is located at Zhongshan Street in Hutou Town, Anxi County. Hanging in the front hall is the plaque "Jiafu Gaofeng" (extremely capable minister with high ambition and moral character, bestowed by Emperor Kangxi). In Husi Village of Hutou Town, next to Junmin Middle School stands Rongcun Book House, or Xianliang (able and virtuous man) Memorial Hall dedicated to Li Guangdi. The walls both inside and outside the main hall are inlaid with marble engravings of poems and texts by Emperor Kangxi, such as *Explanation of Taiji Diagram* and *Poem on Inspecting the Ziyahe River Dam Construction*. On the right of the hall is a stone pavilion with a stele carrying Emperor Yongzheng's *Sacrificial Rites Essay*, praising Li Guangdi as a model of perfection for his era.

贤良祠内的李光地塑像。（刘伯怡 摄）

The statue of Li Guangdi in Xianliang Memorial Hall. (Photo by Liu Boyi)

泉南佛国，桑莲法界——开元寺

Kaiyuan Temple: Sanglian Dharmadhatu in Quanzhou

走向城市的佛教丛林

The Buddhist Temples Going to the City

莲花道场：黄守恭“舍园为寺”

Lotus Buddhist Temple: Huang Shougong Donated His Garden to the Temple

佛陀的圣殿

The Sacred Temple of Buddhas

众塔之下的守望

Overwatching Under the Pagodas

俯瞰开元寺。（陈英杰 摄）
The aerial view of Kaiyuan Temple. (Photo by Chen Yingjie)

泉州开元寺创建于唐垂拱二年（686），位于泉州子城西门外，南临城内东西向主街道，是福建现存规模最大的佛教寺院建筑群，也是宋元时期泉州规模最大、官方地位最突出的佛教寺院。开元寺坐北朝南，由中路主体建筑群、东西石塔及东西两翼附属建筑群等组成，占地面积约78,000平方米，规模雄伟，气势恢宏。

开元寺的寺院经济及多元文化遗迹反映出宋元海洋贸易带给泉州的经济繁荣和文化共存特征。与开元寺相关联的地方统治者、僧侣、地方大族等人群曾对宋元泉州地方社会经济和海洋贸易做出重要贡献。寺内留存有许多珍贵的多元宗教建筑构件，体现了东西方文明在宗教、建筑与艺术文化等方面的交融和多元共存，使我们时至今日仍可感受到当时作为东方第一大港的泉州城内各国人群往来和文化交流互鉴的盛况。

Built in 686 in the Tang Dynasty, Kaiyuan Temple sits outside of the West Gate of Quanzhou's Zicheng (minor wall), bounded by the east-to-west thoroughfare on the south. It is the largest extant Buddhist temple complex in Fujian Province. In the Song and Yuan Dynasties, it was the largest and most prominent official Buddhist temple in Quanzhou. Facing southward, Kaiyuan Temple comprises the central building complex, the east and west stone pagodas, and the eastern and western ancillary buildings. It covers an area of about 78,000 square meters and presents a magnificent and overwhelming view.

Kaiyuan Temple's economic and diverse cultural relics reflect the economic prosperity and the fusion of diverse cultures of Quanzhou in the Song and Yuan Dynasties. Local governors, monks and clans made significant contributions to the city's socio-economic development and maritime trade in the Song and Yuan periods. Precious multi-religious architectural components preserved in the temple reflect the exchanges and coexistence of Eastern and Western civilizations in religion, architecture, art, and culture, which remind us of Quanzhou's glory as the largest port in the East where people and cultures met.

走向城市的佛教丛林

泉州素有“泉南佛国”之称，朱熹更是为泉州开元寺写下“此地古称佛国，满街都是圣人”的联句。历史上，佛教和名山结下不解之缘，有“天下名山僧占多”的说法。然而，这些名山在成名之前多是人迹罕至的荒山，因历代高僧与信众的长期经营才造就了以佛教文化为基底的人文景观，正所谓寺因山而建，山因寺而名。

The Buddhist Temples Going to the City

Quanzhou has been known as "Quannan Buddha City" for its rich Buddhist culture. Zhu Xi once penned a couplet "This place was once a Buddha city, where sacred people can be seen everywhere on the streets". Historically, Buddhism and famous mountains have an inseparable relationship, and there is a saying that "Most of the famous mountains in the world are occupied by monks." However, these mountains were mostly neglected before the long-term management of monks and their believers, creating a humanistic landscape based on the Buddhist culture. Another saying goes, "The temple was built on the mountains. The mountains became, in turn, famous because of the temple."

朱熹为开元寺所题联句。（成冬冬 摄）

The couplet written by Zhu Xi for Kaiyuan Temple. (Photo by Cheng Dongdong)

早在西晋太康九年（288），南安丰州便建有延福寺，这是佛教传入泉州的重要标志。南朝陈文帝天嘉三年（562）更有印度弘法僧拘那罗陀来到延福寺翻译《金刚经》的记载。当时拘那罗陀由丰州梁安港登岸，准备换乘大船返回故乡。受泉州太守及信众的挽留，拘那罗陀一边等待季风的到来，一边在丰州九日山下的延福寺翻译《金刚经》。拘那罗陀也成为现存文献中出现的第一位到访泉州的外国人。

佛教自西晋传入泉州后，在隋唐五代时期得到迅速发展。这一时期泉州的寺院林立，高僧辈出，佛教中的华严宗、法相宗、唯识宗、净土宗、天台宗、密宗、禅宗等各宗派也在泉州传播开来。晋江龙山寺、泉州开元寺、南安雪峰寺、惠安法华寺、德化灵鹫岩寺、永春云峰寺等寺庙得以创建。其他如南安五峰山也有僧人住山修行，唐代僧人道岑居于一片瓦，又有僧人于山上白云岩、狮子岩、觉海岩等处居住修行。

As early as in 288 of the Western Jin Dynasty (265—317), Yanfu Temple was built in Fengzhou, Nan'an City, symbolizing the introduction of Buddhism to Quanzhou. In 562 of the Northern and Southern Dynasties, a record showed that the Indian monk, Gunarata, came to Yanfu Temple to translate *The Diamond Sutra*. At that time, Gunarata disembarked from Liang'an Port in Fengzhou and was about to return to his hometown by large boat. However, the monk was persuaded to stay by the Prefect of Quanzhou and believers in Buddhism. While waiting for the monsoon, he translated *The Diamond Sutra* at Yanfu Temple. Gunarata thus became the first foreigner to visit Quanzhou as recorded in the extant literature.

Buddhism was introduced to Quanzhou in the Western Jin Dynasty and rapidly gained prominence in the Sui, Tang, and Five Dynasties. During this period, Quanzhou became home to numerous monasteries, monks, and various sects of Buddhism such as Huayan Sect, Dharma Character Sect, Vijnanavada, Pure Land Buddhism, Tiantai Sect, Tantric Sect, and Zen Buddhism. Therefore, a number of temples were built in this period, such as Longshan Temple in Jinjiang, Kaiyuan Temple in Quanzhou, Xuefeng Temple in Nan'an, Fahua Temple in Hui'an, Lingjiuyan Temple in Dehua, and Yunfeng Temple in Yongchun. Monks also resided and practiced on Wufeng Mountain in Nan'an. In the Tang Dynasty, the monk Daocen lived at Yipianwa Temple, and other monks explored their spirtual paths to Buddhism near Baiyun Rock, Shizi Rock, Juehai Rock, etc.

延福寺是泉州最早的寺庙。（李芸生 摄）
Yanfu Temple is the first temple in Quanzhou. (Photo by Li Yunsheng)

在南安丰州皇冠山古墓群中曾出土大量南朝时期的模印花纹砖，其中就有许多僧侣、供养人等形象的人物画像砖，这也反映出早期佛教文化在泉州传播的历史。（成冬冬 摄）

In the ancient tomb complex of Crown Hill in Fengzhou, Nan'an, many mold-printed bricks from the Southern Dynasty period were unearthed, including many bricks with images of monks and providers, which are a proof of the spread of early Buddhist culture in Quanzhou. (Photo by Cheng Dongdong)

泉州开元寺创建时的位置与泉州当时的行政中心南安丰州还有一定的距离，然而，随着唐代泉州行政中心的东移和泉州子城的营建，开元寺便毗邻唐代子城的西门肃清门；五代时期留从效拓建罗城，使城市面积扩大了近 7 倍，开元寺也被纳入城中。

When it was founded, Kaiyuan Temple stood at a certain distance from Fengzhou, Nan'an, the administrative center of Quanzhou. However, with the eastward shift of the administrative center of Quanzhou and the building of Zicheng in the Tang Dynasty, the temple was adjacent to the West Gate (Suqing Gate) of Zicheng. During the Five Dynasties period, the temple became an integral part of the city when it underwent significant expansion—nearly sevenfold—under the governance of Governor Liu Congxiao.

与开元寺齐名的泉州都市佛教丛林有承天寺、崇福寺等。（成冬冬 摄）

Other Quanzhou Buddhist temples ranked with Kaiyuan Temple including Chengtian Temple, Chongfu Temple, etc. (Photo by Cheng Dongdong)

莲花道场：黄守恭“舍园为寺”

中古时期崇佛之风日盛，士族与地方富商常将自己的家宅捐献出来建造佛寺，逐渐形成了“舍宅为寺”的传统。关于开元寺的创寺因缘，有一个美好的传说。相传其寺址最初为泉州富商黄守恭所经营的一片大桑园，黄守恭梦见一僧人向他乞地为寺，黄守恭答道：“须树产白莲乃可。”僧人称谢，过了两天，黄家的桑树上竟然开出了白莲，黄守恭遂舍园建寺。

因有此传说，该寺最初被命名为莲花寺。唐代黄滔《泉州开元寺佛殿碑记》曾载，“垂拱二年，郡儒黄守恭桑树吐白莲花，舍为莲花道场”，可见该寺在创寺之初为净土宗道场。

现在开元寺大雄宝殿悬有“桑莲法界”匾额，正记录与印证着“桑树开白莲”这一传说。（成冬冬 摄）
A plaque of "Sanglian Dharma Field" hanging in the Mahavira Hall of Kaiyuan Temple is a record and proof of the legend of "Mulberry trees bloom with lotus". (Photo by Cheng Dongdong)

Lotus Buddhist Temple: Huang Shougong Donated His Garden to the Temple

In the Middle Ages, the Buddhist culture became more and more popular. The gentry and local merchants often donated their residences to build temples, gradually forming the tradition of "donating homes for temples". There is a legend about the founding of Kaiyuan Temple. It says that the temple site was originally a large mulberry garden run by Huang Shougong, a wealthy merchant in Quanzhou. He dreamed of a monk who begged him for the garden to build a temple. Huang Shougong replied, "I shall donate the garden if lotuses grew on my mulberry trees". The monk thanked him. Two days later, lotuses bloomed unexpectedly on his mulberry trees. True to his words, Huang Shougong donated the garden to the temple.

The temple was originally named Lotus Temple according to this legend. In the Tang Dynasty, Huang Tao's work, *Inscription Records of Buddhist Halls in Quanzhou Kaiyuan Temple* recorded: "In 686, lotuses bloomed on mulberry trees in Huang Shougong's residence. To honor his promise, he donated the garden as the Lotus Buddhist Rite", which showed that the temple belonged to the Pure Land Sect at the beginning of its foundation.

开元寺大雄宝殿西侧还保留有一株 1,300 多年的古桑树。桑树周边用围墙加以保护，门匾题有“莲香”二字。（陈英杰 摄）

A mulberry tree of more than 1,300 years old is on the west side of the Mahavira Hall in Kaiyuan Temple. The mulberry tree is protected by a wall with a door plaque inscribed with the Chinese characters " 莲香 " (Lotus Fragrance). (Photo by Chen Yingjie)

武周长寿元年（692），莲花寺改称兴教寺，神龙元年（705）更名龙兴寺。开元二十六年（738），唐玄宗敕令天下诸州各建一寺，以年号为名，开元寺因此得名并沿用至今。

追至宋代，随着泉州海外贸易的发展，开元寺僧人与信众积聚起大量的财富，寺院也得到进一步发展，香火更盛。彼时，开元寺作为闽南第一丛林，其下有支院一百二十所。元至元二十二年（1285），僧录刘鉴义向当时的福建行省长官伯颜奏请并经朝廷批准，将所有支院与开元寺合为一寺，并赐额“敕大开元万寿禅寺”。经此，开元寺禅风远播，衲子竞集。此后的四十年，开元寺进入鼎盛时期，寺内有僧人一千多名，寺志中称“食常万指”。

In 692 of the Tang Dynasty, the Lotus Temple was renamed Xingjiao Temple, and Longxing Temple in 705. In 738, Emperor Xuanzong of the Tang Dynasty decreed every state would build a temple with the name of his reign title, thus the name of Kaiyuan Temple was given and has been kept till now.

In the Song Dynasty, a large amount of wealth was accumulated by the monks and believers of Kaiyuan Temple with the development of the overseas trade in Quanzhou. Therefore, the temple was further developed and attracted more followers. At that time, Kaiyuan Temple, the top one in Southern Fujian, boasted 120 branch temples. In 1285 of the Yuan Dynasty, Liu Jianyi, a monk's registrar, petitioned to the governor of Fujian Province, Bo Yan, to consolidate all the branch temples into one unified temple, and granted the title "The Great Kaiyuan Longevity Zen Temple". After that, the influence of Kaiyuan Temple spread far and wide, and the monks gathered from afar. The following four decades witnessed Kaiyuan Temple's heyday, with more than 1,000 monks, and the temple journal said that there were "often 1,000 eaters".

“敕大开元万寿禅寺”匾额。（成冬冬 摄）
The plaque of "The Great Kaiyuan Longevity Zen Temple". (Photo by Cheng Dongdong)

佛陀的圣殿

泉州开元寺的寺院格局为坐北朝南，中轴线主要建筑自南向北依次为紫云屏、天王殿与拜亭、拜庭及东西廊、大雄宝殿、甘露戒坛、藏经阁及其东侧的檀越祠。寺院东翼有东塔镇国塔、准提禅寺（小开元寺），西翼有西塔仁寿塔、水陆寺与功德堂。开元寺南北长 260 米，东西宽 300 米，占地面积 78,000 平方米。

开元寺天王殿悬有“紫云”匾额，相传建寺之初，时有紫云盖地之瑞，因以得名。前方照壁名为“紫云屏”。紫云屏始建于明万历年间，后于天启年间进行重修。

天王殿前方照壁墙中嵌有“紫云屏”隶书石刻，为明万历四年（1576）泉州书法家陈于王所写。（艾罗斯 摄）

In front of the Devaraja Hall, there is a stone inscription of “Ziyun (Purple Clouds) Shield” in the official script, written by Chen Yuwang, a calligrapher from Quanzhou in 1576. (Photo by Heros Di Bartolomeo)

The Sacred Temple of Buddhas

Kaiyuan Temple is facing south, with the main buildings in the central axis from south to north including Ziyun Shield, the Devaraja Hall and Worship Pavilion, Worship Courtyard, East and West Corridors, the Mahavira Hall, Ganlu Precept Altar, Sutra Depository and Tanyue Hall on its east side. In the east wing of the temple are the East Pagoda (Zhenguo Pagoda) and Zhunti Zen Temple (small Kaiyuan Temple), and in the west wing, the West Pagoda (Renshou Pagoda), the Water-Land Temple and the Hall of Merit. Kaiyuan Temple is 260 meters long and 300 meters wide, with a coverage of 78,000 square meters.

There is a “Ziyun(Purple Clouds)” plaque hanging in the Devaraja Hall of the temple, and the screen wall was named “Ziyun Shield”. It came from a legend that purple clouds covered the sky when the temple was built, showing an auspicious view. The screen wall was built during 1573 and 1620 and rebuilt during 1621 and 1627 of the Ming Dynasty.

天王殿始建于唐垂拱二年（686），为单檐硬山顶，面阔五间，进深三间。殿中石柱承袭了唐代风格，呈梭状，柱础则具有宋代特征，为覆盆状。殿中两侧依佛教密宗规制分置塑像各一，分别为密迹金刚与梵王，这与一般寺庙天王殿中所塑的风调雨顺四大天王有较大差别。殿后附有拜亭一座，为面阔、进深各一间的卷棚歇山顶式建筑，俗称“拜香亭”。

The Devaraja Hall, constructed during the Tang Dynasty in 686, is five-*chien* wide and three-*chien* deep and with a single-eave gabled roof. The stone pillars in the hall are shuttle-shaped inherited the style of the Tang Dynasty, and the pillar bases are basin-shaped in the style of the Song Dynasty. Following the Buddhist Tantric rules, the hall has one statue on each side, respectively the Tantric Vajrba and King Brahma, which is quite different from the four Devarajas in the Devaraja Hall of other temples. There is a worship pavilion attached to the hall, which is a one-*chien* wide and one-*chien* deep building with a round ridge saddled roof, commonly known as "The Worship Incense Pavilion".

开元寺天王殿。（刘宝生 摄）
The Devaraja Hall of Kaiyuan Temple. (Photo by Liu Baosheng)

拜庭是连接天王殿与大雄宝殿的庭院，可供寺僧与信众聚集所用，两翼有长廊回护。在拜庭两侧分别有自唐代至明代建造的陀罗尼石经幢、宝箧印经塔、窣堵波式塔与舍利塔等，拜庭中还有石香炉。关于拜庭不生杂草的缘故，开元寺寺志中有“垂云刹草”的说法，“尝有紫云覆寺至地，至今凡草不生其庭”。

大雄宝殿及其前方的拜庭。（成冬冬 摄）
The Mahavira Hall and the Worship Courtyard in its front. (Photo by Cheng Dongdong)

Connecting the Devaraja Hall and the Mahavira Hall, the Worship Courtyard serves as a gathering place for monks and worshipers. It is flanked by long corridors. On both sides of the Worship Courtyard are the stone Dharana sutra pillars, Hōkyōintō, the stūpa pagodas, and Sarira pagodas built from the Tang Dynasty to the Ming Dynasty, as well as the stone incense burner. The temple's annals recount a tale known as "Hanging Clouds Removed Weeds". According to this legend, purple clouds once enveloped the courtyard, preventing weeds from growing.

大雄宝殿始建于唐垂拱二年（686），明崇祯十年（1637）右参政、按察使曾樱与福建总兵郑芝龙捐赀重修，并将木头柱子全部换为石柱，使之避免南方潮湿天气中白蚁的侵蚀。大雄宝殿为木构抬梁式建筑，重檐歇山顶，面阔九间，进深九间，根据九开间柱网布局，故而又称“百柱殿”。为使殿内有足够的空间供奉佛像，匠师们巧妙运用了减柱结构方式，于殿中减去两列 14 根石柱，因此大殿实际上只有 86 根石柱。

大雄宝殿气势恢宏。（刘宝生 摄）
The Mahavira Hall is magnificent and impressive. (Photo by Liu Baosheng)

The Mahavira Hall was built in 686 of the Tang Dynasty. In 1637 of the Ming Dynasty, Zeng Ying, the Right Counselor and Surveillance Commissioner, and Zheng Zhilong, the Commander-in-Chief of Fujian, donated money to rebuild it. They replaced all the wooden pillars with stone ones to prevent termite damage in the humid weather in Southern China. The Mahavira Hall features wooden building with beams, double eaves and a saddle roof. It is nine-*chien* wide and nine-*chien* deep, adhering to the layout of the nine-*chien* pillar network, so also known as the "One-Hundred-Pillar Hall". To make enough space for the Buddha statues, the craftsmen made use of the "reducing pillar" method and removed away14 stone pillars in the hall. Finally, only 86 stone pillars were left.

大雄宝殿内以密宗规制供奉着五方佛（又称五智如来），正中为毗卢遮那佛，东侧自右向左为东方香积世界阿閦佛、南方欢喜世界宝生佛，西侧自右向左为西方极乐世界阿弥陀佛、北方莲花世界不空成就佛。殿中佛像法相庄严，令人肃然起敬。大殿中令人赞叹的还有五方佛像前两排石柱与梁架接合处的斗拱所装饰的 24 尊迦陵频伽。她们或执管弦丝竹，或捧文房四宝，既起到承担支撑梁架结构的作用，又具有极高的艺术价值，这在中国传统木构建筑中也是极为罕见的。

大雄宝殿中的五方佛。（陈英杰 摄）
The Five Dhyani Buddhas in the Mahavira Hall. (Photo by Chen Yingjie)

According to the Tantric standard, the Mahavira Hall enshrines the Five Dhyani Buddhas. In the middle is Vairocana. In the east, from right to left, are Aksobhya Buddha in the oriental incense accumulation world and Ratnasambhava in the southern joy world. In the west, from right to left, are Amitabha Buddha in the western Sukhavati and Amogha-siddhi in the northern lotus world. The Buddha statues in the hall are solemn and awe-inspiring. In the Mahavira hall, there are also 24 Kalavinkas decorated on the bracket sets at the junction of the first two rows of stone columns and the beam frame of the Five Dhyani Buddhas. They either hold musical instruments, or the four treasures of the study, not only serving to support the beam structure, but also having great artistic value, which is extremely rare in traditional Chinese wooden buildings.

斗拱上装饰的 24 尊迦陵频伽。（陈英杰 摄）
The 24 Kalavinkas decorated on the bracket sets. (Photo by Chen Yingjie)

大殿月台须弥座束腰处有 73 幅狮子与人面狮身的辉绿岩浮雕，这与南印度朱罗时期的印度教寺院里的人面狮身石刻风格十分相似。大殿后廊檐还有两根印度教十六角形辉绿岩石柱，柱身各有 12 幅圆浮雕。在这 24 幅雕刻图像中有 8 幅与古代印度教神话故事相关，其内容来源于印度著名史诗《摩诃婆罗多》《罗摩衍那》。柱身雕刻有湿婆苦行立像、毗湿奴骑坐金翅鸟、毗湿奴和他的两位妻子、人狮毗湿奴、阎摩那河七女出浴、吹笛子的克里希那、克里希那与阿周树、象鳄争斗、两个摔跤手等图像；其他则是中国传统吉祥图案，如双狮戏球、双凤衔瑞草以及吉祥花卉与动物图案等。中印两种不同的艺术风格同处一根石柱上，也是不同文化背景的人们和谐相处的一个缩影。这些石构件都是明末重修寺院时从废弃的元代印度教寺庙中移来再利用的，展示出开元寺的开放、包容以及泉州社会文化的繁荣与活力。

月台束腰处狮子与人面狮身浮雕。（成冬冬 摄）
Reliefs of lions and sphinxes at the waist of the platform. (Photo by Cheng Dongdong)

There are 73 diabase reliefs of lions and sphinxes at the waist of the Sumeru pedestal the platform of the Mahavira Hall, which resemble the sphinxes carved in the Hindu monasteries of the Jura period in Southern India. Positioned on the eaves of the rear porch, two Hindu hexagonal diabase pillars feature 12 round reliefs each. 8 of the 24 carved images depict scenes from ancient Hindu mythologies, drawing inspiration from the famous Indian epics *Mahabharata* and *Ramayana*. The pillars' bodies are carved with images of Shiva performing austerities, Vishnu riding on golden-winged birds, Vishnu and his two wives, Narasimha, and Vishnu, seven women bathing in the river Yamana, Krishna playing the flute, Krishna and A Chau Tree, battle of elephants and alligators, two wrestlers, etc. Other pictures are traditional Chinese auspicious motifs, such as two lions playing with a ball, two phoenixes carrying the auspicious grass, and auspicious floral and animal motifs. The two different artistic styles of China and India are on the same stone pillar, a microcosm of how people from different cultural backgrounds lived together in harmony. These stone elements were relocated and reused from an abandoned Yuan Dynasty Hindu temple during Kaiyuan Temple's restoration in the late Ming Dynasty, demonstrating its openness and inclusiveness, as well as the prosperity and vitality of Quanzhou's society and culture.

大雄宝殿后廊印度教十六角形辉绿岩石柱。（成冬冬 摄）
Hindu hexadecagon diabase pillars in the back corridor of the Mahavira Hall. (Photo by Cheng Dongdong)

戒坛是古代佛教僧侣举行隆重受戒仪式的专门场所。开元寺甘露戒坛建于北宋天禧三年（1019），据寺志载：“甘露戒坛，在大殿之后。先是唐时，其地常降甘露，僧行昭因浚甘露井。宋天禧三年朝例普度，僧始筑戒坛。”南宋建炎二年（1128），寺僧敦炤大师认为原来的戒坛不符古制，又依《南山图经》中的戒坛形制进行改建。现戒坛木构部分为康熙五年（1666）重修，殿中存有重建纪事碑记，在戒坛北侧廊下还有甘露井。

甘露戒坛为五重檐八角攒尖顶式，坛顶作八角圆形蜘蛛结网藻井。坛台为平面四方五层台座，象征着五分法身，第五层供奉着明代木雕卢舍那佛坐像，其下为须弥座莲花台，每一叶莲花瓣上各刻有一尊佛像，计 1,000 尊，故又称“千佛莲台”；释迦牟尼佛、阿弥陀佛、千手千眼观音、菩萨、韦驮、弥勒、金刚诸神自上而下层层围护，共计 27 尊。

甘露戒坛的形制与古代佛教经典所记规制高度吻合，是佛教建筑发展史的珍贵物证。（刘宝生 摄）
Ganlu Precept Altar's shape and structure are highly consistent with the rules recorded in ancient Buddhist classics, making the altar precious evidence of the history of Buddhist architecture development. (Photo by Liu Baosheng)

Precept Altar is a sacred site for monks to hold grand preceptorship ceremonies in ancient times. Ganlu (Ganlu means "sweet dew" in Chinese) Precept Altar was built in 1019 of the Northern Song Dynasty. According to the temple's annals, "Ganlu Precept Altar was located behind the Mahavira Hall. In the Tang Dynasty, sweet dew often drop here, and monk Xingzhao dredged the Ganlu Well. In 1019 of the Northern Song Dynasty, monks began to build the altar to hold the regular assembly." In 1128 of the Southern Song Dynasty, Master Dunzhao, a monk of the temple, thought that the original altar did not conform to the ancient system and rebuilt it according to the shape and structure of the altar described in *The Nanshan Tujing*. The wooden part of the present altar was rebuilt in 1666. There is a stele commemorating the reconstruction in the hall. Under the corridor to the north of the altar lies the Ganlu Well.

Ganlu Precept Altar is a building with five eaves and an octagonal pointed roof. The altar platform is a flat square and five-layer pedestal, symbolizing the five types of the Dharma body. The fifth layer is dedicated to the wood sitting statue of Locana Buddha carved in the Ming Dynasty. He is sitting on the Sumeru Lotus Pedestal. On each petal is engraved a Buddha statue, 1,000 statues in all, also known as "A Thousand Buddhas Lotus Platform". The standing statues of Sakyamuni and Amitabha, the thousand-hand-thousand-eye Kuan Yin, the Bodhisattvas, Vedas, Maitreya, and vajra deities are surrounded by layers from top to bottom, 27 statues in all.

甘露戒坛内柱头及补间铺作有 24 尊手执琵琶、二弦、洞箫、响板等南音乐器的迦陵频伽，其身姿如敦煌飞天，这在我国寺庙戒坛中也是独具特色的。（陈英杰 摄）

There are 24 Kalavinkas playing Nanyin musical instruments such as pipa, two-stringed fiddles, Chinese Bamboo Xiao, ringing board in the pillar head between the fillings and intercolumnar bracket sets in Ganlu Precept Altar. Their postures resemble the flying apsaras in Dunhuang, which is unique in China's temple preceptors. (Photo by Chen Yingjie)

藏经阁是佛寺中存放经书的场所。开元寺藏经阁始建于元至元二十年（1283），现存建筑为 1925 年改建的水泥仿木楼阁结构。

檀越祠旧为伽蓝祠，在法堂之左，元代至元间，由寺僧妙恩所建。该祠为四进硬山顶带东护厝的砖木石混合建筑，明清以降屡有修缮，祠内有碑以纪其事。

藏经阁内收藏有宋、元、明版纸本经书，以及贝叶经、血经等珍贵的佛教经书。（成冬冬 摄）

The Sutra Depository collects paper scriptures from the Song, Yuan and Ming Dynasties, as well as precious Buddhist scriptures such as the palm leaf manuscripts and blood manuscripts. (Photo by Cheng Dongdong)

The Sutra Depository serves as a repository for sacred scriptures within a Buddhist temple. It was first built in 1283 of the Yuan Dynasty. In 1925, this existing cement was reconstructed in imitation of a wooden structure.

Tanyue Hall, formerly known as the Qielan Hall, was built by the monk Miao'en during 1264 and 1294 of the Yuan Dynasty. Positioned on the left side of the Dharma Hall, this hall is a four-hall building with a gabbled roof, which was made of brick, wood and stone, and with an east guard house. It has been repaired since the Ming and Qing Dynasties. There is a monument in the hall to record its events.

为感念黄守恭对开元寺的贡献，于今藏经阁东侧建祠以纪念檀越主黄守恭。（成冬冬 摄）
To commemorate Huang Shougong for his contribution to Kaiyuan Temple, a memorial hall named Tanyue Hall was built on the east side of the present Sutra Depository. (Photo by Cheng Dongdong)

众塔之下的守望

塔是佛教的产物，起源于印度，在梵文中称Stupa，巴利文则称为Thupo，其原意为“积聚”，即积土石而成，或谓佛的福德积聚于此，有坟冢之意，中文译作塔婆、浮屠、佛图等。

佛教初传中国时，佛寺受印度的影响，以塔为中心在其周围建造殿堂与僧舍。公元5世纪以后，塔在中国佛寺中的格局位置开始发生改变——殿堂逐渐成为佛寺的主要建筑，而塔的位置则由全寺的中心演变为左右分列于殿前，或于主殿院落前方两侧分立塔院，也有将佛塔移于寺外另建的。

泉州开元寺双塔的塔院布局体现了佛寺格局变革的早期特征，具有标本性价值。（陈英杰 摄）
The twin-pagoda layout, such as the two pagodas of Kaiyuan Temple in Quanzhou, embodies the early changes of the Buddhist temple, which has great value. (Photo by Chen Yingjie)

Overwatching Under the Pagodas

The pagoda is associated with Buddhism, originating from India. It is derived from the Sanskrit word Stupa or the Pali word Thupo, both of which signify "accumulation". It refers to the mound of earth and stones that was built to enshrine the relics or honor the achievements of a Buddha or a saint. In Chinese, it is interpreted as 塔婆 (Tapa), 浮屠 (Fudo), 佛图 (Buddha Figure), etc.

When Buddhism was first introduced to China, temples in the country were influenced by Indian temples. People usually built halls and monasteries with pagodas as the center. But, after the 5th century AD, the position of pagodas in Chinese temples began to change. Halls gradually became the main structures of temples, while the position of pagodas evolved from the center to both sides in front of the halls, or in front of the courtyard of the main hall one pagoda stood on each side. Sometimes the pagodas were even built outside the temple.

在泉州民间一直流传着这么一句话：“站如东西塔，坐如老君岩，躺如洛阳桥。”

开元寺东塔名为镇国塔，“唐咸亨文偁师始作木塔，凡五级。……咸通六年（865），木塔成，赐名镇国”。北宋天禧中东塔改做十三级木塔，南宋宝庆三年（1227）改建为七层砖塔，嘉熙二年至淳祐十年（1238—1250）重建时改为石塔。

东塔代表着东方娑婆世界，其塔身外壁每层雕有佛像 16 尊，五层共 80 尊。造像自下而上分别依照人乘、天乘、声闻乘、缘觉乘、菩萨乘的佛教五乘佛法排列，分别为诸天神将、罗汉、高僧、菩萨、佛尊。

东塔须弥座束腰处有浮雕 40 幅，其中 37 幅为释迦牟尼生前因缘、出世后的行迹以及佛教中的譬喻故事等为主要内容的《佛本生经》故事图像。

就东塔的建造工艺来看，其塔壁一顺多丁的砌筑方式以及塔身收分、门龛错位、分段接柱等建造方式，不仅增强了塔身的稳定性，使之更为美观，还提高了抗震能力，体现了古代造塔工匠的非凡智慧。

镇国塔为五层八角仿阁楼式石塔，通高 48.27 米，塔由塔座、塔身、塔顶、塔刹四部分组成，塔中为花岗岩块石叠砌的八角形塔心柱，自塔底直达塔顶。（刘宝生 摄）

Zhenguo Pagoda stands 48.27 meters high and is composed of four parts: the base, the body, the top, and the spire. In it an octagonal pagoda center column made of granites reaches from the bottom to the top of the pagoda. (Photo by Liu Baosheng)

In Quanzhou, a saying goes: "One must stand as upright as the East and West Pagodas, sit as stable as the Statue of Lao Tze, and lie down as unyielding as Luoyang Bridge."

The East Pagoda also known as Zhenguo Pagoda, which can be explained by such record: "During 670 and 674 of the Tang Dynasty, Master Wencheng initiated the construction of a five-storey wooden pagoda... However, it wasn't until 865 that the wooden pagoda was finally completed, bearing the name Zhenguo." It was later rebuilt several times: as a thirteen-storey wooden pagoda between 1017 and 1021 of the Northern Song Dynasty, as a seven-storey brick pagoda in 1227 of the Southern Song Dynasty, and as a stone pagoda from 1238 to 1250.

The East Pagoda represents the Oriental Saha World, with 16 Buddha statues carved on the outer walls of each floor, a total of 80 statues on five floors. Following the Law of Five Realms (manusya-yāna, deva-yāna, Sravakayana, pratyeka-buddha-yāna, bodhisattva-yana), the statues are arranged from bottom to top: all heavenly divine generals, Buddhism arhats, accomplished monks, the Bodhisattvas, and the Buddhas.

The East Pagoda features 40 reliefs carved around the waist of the Sumeru pedestal, 37 of which depict stories about Jātaka such as the *Buddha's Life Sutra* with Shakyamuni's life, his deeds after birth and various Buddhist parables.

The East Pagoda demonstrates the remarkable skill and ingenuity of the ancient pagoda builders. Its construction process invoked the masonry of the walls and the body of the pagoda, the misalignment of the door niche, the segmentation of the column and other construction methods, not only enhance the stability and beauty of the pagoda but also improve its anti-seismic capability.

镇国塔外壁的浮雕代表着佛教修行的五种境界以及他们在娑婆世界担负自身修行和普度众生的责任。（刘宝生 摄）

The relief sculptures on the exterior walls of Zhenguo Pagoda represents the five realms of Buddhist practice and their responsibility for their own practice and for delivering all living creatures from torment in the Saha World. (Photo by Liu Baosheng)

西塔名为仁寿塔，始建于五代后梁贞明二年（916），初为七级木塔，原名无量寿塔。北宋时西塔改建为砖塔，南宋绍定元年至嘉熙元年（1228—1237）再改建为石塔。

西塔代表着西方极乐世界，其塔身雕像不同于东塔雕刻的人物有鲜明的尊卑等级观念，在西塔之上主要弘扬众生佛性平等，故每层门龛两侧交互雕刻着神将、信士、圣僧、帝王及菩萨等人物形象。西塔须弥座所雕图案均是中国传统花卉鸟兽图案，有双龙戏珠、双狮戏球、祥花瑞草等浮雕 40 幅。

仁寿塔的规制和建塔工艺与镇国塔相似，高度上略低于镇国塔，通高 45.06 米。（成冬冬 摄）
Renshou Pagoda has a similar structure and construction process as Zhenguo Pagoda, but it is slightly lower, 45.06 meters in height. (Photo by Cheng Dongdong)

The West Pagoda, also known as Renshou Pagoda, was originally called the Longevity Pagoda. A seven-storey wooden pagoda was first built in 916. In the Northern Song Dynasty, it was converted into a brick pagoda. From 1228 to 1237 of the Southern Song Dynasty, it was reconstructed into a stone pagoda.

The West Pagoda symbolizes the Western Land of Ultimate Bliss, where all beings have the same Buddha nature. Unlike the East Pagoda, which has figures of different ranks and statuses, on both sides of the door niche at each layer of the West Pagoda were carved the gods, believers, holy monks, emperors and bodhisattvas and other figures. The motifs carved on the Sumeru pedestal of the West Pagoda are all traditional Chinese floral, bird and animal motifs, with 40 relief carvings of double dragons playing with a pearl, double lions playing with a ball, auspicious flowers and grass, etc.

镇国塔第 2 层和仁寿塔第 4 层分别雕刻有唐三藏和猴行者。（成冬冬 摄）
The 2nd floor of Zhenguo Pagoda and the 4th floor of Renshou Pagoda were respectively carved with Tang Sanzang and Ascetic Sun. (Photo by Cheng Dongdong)

仁寿塔须弥座浮雕和负塔力士。（成冬冬 摄）
The relief sculptures and the malla carrying pagoda on the Sumeru pedestal of Renshou Pagoda. (Photo by Cheng Dongdong)

开元寺东西塔作为我国现存最高的一对宋代石塔，代表了 13 世纪中国石构建筑技艺的最高水平，不仅是泉州古城的地标，也是中国石构建筑史上的杰出范例。正因东西塔极高的辨识度与广泛的影响力，其形象图案在我国发行的邮票中多次被使用。

开元寺大雄宝殿前有两座宝箧印经塔，因其形似宝箧且内藏印经而得名，为印度密教浮海东渐的产物。传说公元前二世纪古印度阿育王敕建八万四千座塔，其中有 19 座传入中国，故宝箧印经塔又称“阿育王塔”。五代时期吴越王钱弘俶仿效阿育王，建造八万四千座塔。像开元寺这种大型石构宝箧印经塔现仅存于浙闽粤沿海三省，特别是泉州一带尤多。这两座宝箧印经塔高 5.48 米，由基座、塔身、塔顶、塔刹 4 部分组成。方形基座与塔身是宝箧印经塔的基本特征，塔身四面刻龛，雕刻着佛本生故事。塔顶上四角立着山花蕉叶，上面刻有佛陀故事。塔刹形制完整，由覆莲、五重相轮等组成。

开元寺东西塔。（刘贤涛 摄）
The East and West Pagodas of Kaiyuan Temple. (Photo by Liu Xiantao)

As the tallest existing pair of stone pagodas from the Song Dynasty, the East Pagoda and West Pagoda of Kaiyuan Temple represent the superb Chinese stone construction techniques in the 13th century. They are not only landmarks of the ancient city of Quanzhou, but also outstanding examples in the history of Chinese stone architecture. Their distinctive identity and great influence have led to the application of their images to several stamps issued in China.

In front of the Mahavira Hall of Kaiyuan Temple, there are two Hōkyōintō, named for their resemblance to treasure suitcases and the scriptures they contain, which were introduced from Indian Tantra. Legend has it that in the 2nd century B.C., King Ashoka of ancient India built 84,000 pagodas, of which 19 were introduced to China, so the pagodas are also known as Ashoka pagodas. During the Five Dynasties period, King Qian Hongchu of Wuyue Kingdom followed Ashoka's practice and built another 84,000 pagodas. Large stone pagodas such as those two in Kaiyuan Temple now exist only in the coastal provinces like Zhejiang, Fujian, and Guangdong, especially in Quanzhou area. These two pagodas are 5.48 meters high and consist of four parts: the base, the body, the top, and the spire. The square base and body are the basic characteristic of the pagodas. Four sides of the pagodas are carved with niches and stories of the Buddha's life as Bodhisattva for many generations. The tops of the pagodas are decorated with banana leaves On them are carved the story of Buddha. The decoration on the spires consists of an inverted lotus and five wheels, complete in structure and design.

开元寺大雄宝殿前的宋代二塔。（成冬冬 摄）
The two pagodas of the Song Dynasty in front of the Mahavira Hall of Kaiyuan Temple. (Photo by Cheng Dongdong)

东侧宝箧印经塔的塔身四面雕刻有佛本生故事。塔身铭刻有“右南厢梁安家室柳三娘舍钱造宝塔二座同祈平安，绍兴乙丑七月题，王思问舍钱三十贯 乙酉重修”。通过塔身石刻铭文可知该塔建于南宋绍兴十五年(1145)。

1982 年，东侧宝箧印经塔被第九号强台风折断的巨大榕树击倒。人们在灾后清理过程中于石塔基座发现一座八角八面石质经幢，系泉州刺史王继勋于南唐保大四年（946）建造。幢身通高 1.2 米，每面宽 0.19 米，竖刻 76 行文字，主要部分为《佛顶尊胜陀罗尼经》经文。经文为工整的楷书，刻工精细。经幢幢身为石灰岩，是特地从太湖采办而来的湖石，质地较脆，结构细密，吸水性较强。经幢铭文中刻记施舍建幢人的姓名，其中就有许多地方官员，比如“军事左押衙充海路都指挥兼御史大夫陈匡俊”“権利院使刘拯”等官名和机构。这也反映出五代时期地方统治者对海外贸易的重视及泉州海外贸易的发展情况已经需要设立专门的机构并指派专门的官员来负责管理海外贸易。

东侧宝箧印经塔塔身雕刻及铭文。（成冬冬 摄）

The carving and inscription on the body of the Hōkyōintō in the east side of the courtyard of Kaiyuan Temple. (Photo by Cheng Dongdong)

The Hōkyōintō in the east side of the courtyard features carvings depicting the Buddha's life as Bodhisattva on the four sides of the body. The pagoda has the following inscription: "Liu Sanniang of Liang An's family from the right south district of Quanzhou, donated money to build two pagodas praying for peace. Inscribed in lunar July of 1145 of the Southern Song Dynasty. Later, Wang Siwen contributed 30 *guan* of money to rebuild them in 1165". The inscription clearly shows that the pagodas were built in 1145 of the Southern Song Dynasty.

In 1982, the pagoda was knocked down by a huge banyan tree snapped off by typhoon No. 9. During the post-disaster cleanup, an octagonal, eight-sided stone Dharani Sutra pillar was found at the pagoda's base. The pillar was built by Wang Jixun, governor of Quanzhou, in 946 of the Southern Tang Dynasty. Standing at 1.2 meters high and 0.19 meters wide, this elegant pillars bears 76 lines of vertically carved characters. The main part is scripture from *Buddhosnisah Dharani*, which is in neat regular script with fine engraving. Its body is hewn from limestone, a lake stone bought from Taihu Lake, with a brittle texture, fine structure, and high-water absorption. Among the names inscribed on the pillar are many local officials who gave alms to build the pillar, such as Chen Kuangjun, a high-ranking military official, and Liu Zheng, the envoy of *Queliyuan* (an official institute monopolizes certain materials to increase fiscal revenue). This also reflects the importance that local rulers attached to overseas trade during the Five Dynasties period and the development of Quanzhou's overseas trade, which called for specialized institutions and officials to manage overseas trade.

五代王继勋建造的陀罗尼经幢。（成冬冬 摄）
The Dharani Sutra pillar built by Wang Jixun in the Five Dynasties. (Photo by Cheng Dongdong)

人们在清理倒塌的石塔构件时，还于塔下的束腰基座部位发现了银制鎏金的佛雕像、铜镜、铜钱以及唐宋时期的瓷片等物品。尤为引人注意的有宋银鎏金释迦牟尼坐像、宋银鎏金带塔形罩观音立像、宋湖州八菱花形铜镜、宋花蝶纹方形铜镜等。其中宋银鎏金带塔形罩观音立像由葫芦顶神帐、佛像和须弥座三部分组成，在塔形罩外阴刻楷书："泉州右南厢宣明坊女弟子柳三娘，与夫主梁安共舍宝塔一座，永充供奉，合家人口等增延福寿，时绍兴十五年六月□日弟子梁安题"，这也可与宝箧印经塔塔身题刻相印证。而在宋湖州八菱花形铜镜上，还阳文楷书"湖州仪凤桥石家真正一色青铜镜"，这为我们提供了宋代商品往来的一个重要实证。

开元寺拜庭东侧宝箧印经塔中发现的宋银鎏金释迦牟尼坐像及银鎏金带塔形罩观音立像。（成冬冬 摄）
The sitting silver statue of Sakyamuni gilded with gold and the standing silver statue of Kuan Yin gilded with gold and covered with a pagoda-shaped tent from the Song Dynasty, unearthed in the Asoka pagoda in the east side of the Worship Courtyard of Kaiyuan Temple. (Photo by Cheng Dongdong)

When the debris of the collapsed stone pagoda was cleaned up, silver Buddha statues gilded with gold, bronze mirrors, copper coins, and porcelain pieces from the Tang and Song Dynasties were found on the waist base under the pagoda. Some compelling objects from the Song Dynasty include the sitting silver statue of Sakyamuni gilded with gold and the standing silver statue of Kuan Yin gilded with gold and covered with a pogada-shaped tent, the bronze mirror with eight water chestnut flowers from Huzhou, and the square bronze mirror with flower and butterfly patterns. The standing silver statue of Kuan Yin gilded with gold and covered with a pagoda-shaped tent is composed of three parts: the gourd top divine tent, the statue, and the Sumeru pedestal. On the outer side of the pagoda-shaped tent were incised with the characters in the regular script: "Liu Sanniang, a female disciple of Xuanming Lane in the Right South District of Quanzhou, donated to build this pagoda with her husband Liang An. May the family be blessed. These characters were penned by Liang An in lunar June, 1145." This can also be confirmed by the inscription on the pagoda's body. On the bronze mirror with eight water chestnut flowers from Huzhou in the Song Dynasty were incised with the characters in the regular script reads, "Shi Family's true color bronze mirror near Yifeng Bridge, Huzhou", which provides us with important evidence of commodity exchanges during the Song Dynasty.

东侧宝箧印经塔中发现的宋湖州八菱花形铜镜和宋花蝶纹方形铜镜。（成冬冬 摄）

Huzhou bronze mirror with eight water chestnut flowers and the square bronze mirror with flower and butterfly patterns from the Song Dynasty found in the Asoka pagoda in the east side of the Worship Courtyard. (Photo by Cheng Dongdong)

在拜庭西北角及东北角，还分立有两座花岗岩佛顶尊胜陀罗尼经幢。据《佛顶尊胜陀罗尼经》记载，诵读陀罗尼经或建造陀罗尼经幢可消除罪业，这也使得信徒热心捐资建造经幢。位于东北角的石经幢刻于唐代大中八年（854），这也是泉州现存年代最早的石经幢。该幢原非开元寺旧物，1935 年发现于泉州西门吊桥下，1953 年才移至开元寺保存。位于西北角的经幢刻于北宋大中祥符元年（1008），为寺僧元绍所建的水陆寺陀罗尼经幢。现在这两座经幢仅幢身为唐、宋原物，基座和幢顶均为补配。

窣堵波式塔最初是埋葬佛祖释迦牟尼舍利的一种佛教建筑，此后逐渐转变为高僧圆寂后埋藏其舍利的建筑。窣堵波式塔的基本形制是用砖石垒筑圆形或方形的台基，在台基之上建一个球形覆钵，即塔身。塔身中常雕刻佛首形象，塔内一般埋藏有石函或铜函等舍利容器。拜庭东西两侧分立着窣堵波式塔 9 座，其中大多建于明代。

在大雄宝殿后庭，也存有两座南宋时期的窣堵波式塔，东侧塔身刻有铭文：“奉三宝信士刘大亨命工建造宝塔二座，用荐□二亲，资超□界。时嘉定辛未（1211）正月吉日谨题”。

拜庭西北角和东北角的陀罗尼经幢。（成冬冬 摄）
Dharani Sutra pillars in the northwest and the northeast corners of the Worship Courtyard. (Photo by Cheng Dongdong)

Two Buddhosnisah Dharani Sutra pillars made of granites stand in the northwest and northeast corners of the Worship Courtyard. According to *Buddhosnisah Dharani*, chanting Dharani or building Dharani Sutra pillars can eliminate sins, which motivated devotees enthusiastically to donate money to build Dharani Sutra pillars. The stone pillar in the northeast corner was carved in 854 of the Tang Dynasty, which is the earliest surviving stone sutra building in Quanzhou. It was found under the suspension bridge at the West Gate of Quanzhou in 1935 and moved to Kaiyuan Temple in 1953 for preservation. The other pillar was carved in 1008 of the Northern Song Dynasty, and was built by the monk Yuanshao as a Dharani pillar of the Water Land Temple. Now only the bodies of these two sutra pillars are original, and the bases and tops were replenished.

The stūpa pagoda was initially a Buddhist building for burying the sarira of Buddha Shakyamuni and gradually became a building for enshrining eminent monks' sariras. Its basic form is a round or square masonry base, with a spherical mantle on top, i.e., the pagoda body. It is often carved with the image of Buddha's head, and the pagoda is usually buried with stone or copper sarira containers. On the east and west sides of the Worship Courtyard are nine stūpa pagodas, most of which were built in the Ming Dynasty.

In the backyard of the Mahavira Hall, there are also two stūpa pagodas of the Southern Song Dynasty. The eastern pagoda has an inscription that reads "Liu Daheng, a believer of Triratna (the Buddha, the dharma, the sangha), initiated the construction of two pagodas. May the benefit extend to his parents and the donation transcend the realms. Inscribed on the auspicious day of lunar January, 1211."

大雄宝殿后庭的窣堵波式塔。（成冬冬 摄）
The Stūpa pagodas in the backyard of the Mahavira Hall. (Photo by Cheng Dongdong)

从开元寺历代营建理念与工艺来看，其设计科学、体量宏伟、雕艺精湛、内涵丰富，也从侧面反映出 13 世纪时泉州作为国家指定的国际港口拥有先进的建筑技术、完整的工程组织、强大的社会动员能力以及雄厚的经济实力。

开元寺作为闽南地区香火十分旺盛的佛教寺院，也一直与周边居民保持着良好的互动。每年开元寺会举行许多大型法会，比如每个月农历二十六日的勤佛日，而像元宵节、佛诞日、中元节等代表性佛事盛典，寺僧也都会举行法会。从这些活动中我们也可以看出宗教传统和民间信俗在泉州得到了良好的传承与延续。

香火旺盛的开元寺。（刘宝生 摄）
Kaiyuan Temple with busy crowds and worshipers. (Photo by Liu Baosheng)

Kaiyuan Temple showcases the scientific design, grand scale, exquisite carving skills, and rich content. It also reflects the advanced construction technology, complete engineering organization, great social mobilization ability and economic strength of Quanzhou as a nationally designated international port in the 13th century.

As a Buddhist temple with a very strong worship culture in Southern Fujian, Kaiyuan Temple has also maintained good interaction with neighboring residents. Every year, Kaiyuan Temple holds many significant pujas, such as that on the 26th day of each lunar month. The monks also hold pujias in other representative Buddhist feasts like the Lantern Festival, the Buddha's Birthday, and the Hungry Ghost Festival (a traditional Buddhist and Taoist festival held in certain East Asian countries). These events demonstrate the continuity of religious traditions and folk beliefs in Quanzhou.

开元寺勤佛日活动。（田米 摄）
The activities on Buddhist Devotion Day in Kaiyuan Temple. (Photo by Tian Mi)

老子雕像，道法自然——老君岩造像

The Stone Statue of Lao Tze: Holding the Law of the Tao Is Its Being What It Is

泉州清源山老君岩造像是道家学说创始人老子的石雕像。这一巨大的石雕像是宋代泉州官方主流意识形态的象征，展现了当时雄厚的社会财富，体现了泉州港口依托农业帝国的独特历史文脉。老君岩造像显示了当时泉州道教盛行，民间信仰多元化和儒、道、释并存的社会意识，也反映出泉州作为世界海洋贸易中心多元、活跃的文化特征和港口的繁荣成就。

位于泉州北郊的清源山不仅是道教名山，还有佛教和伊斯兰教的史迹。（李芸生 摄）

Qingyuan Mountain, located in the northern suburbs of Quanzhou, is not only a famous Taoist mountain, but also has Buddhist and Islamic historical relics. (Photo by Li Yunsheng)

The Stone Statue of Lao Tze (also Lao-Tzu or Lao-Tze) in Qingyuan Mountain in Quanzhou was carved to commemorate Lao Tze, the founder of Taoism. It was the symbol of Quanzhou's official mainstream ideology in the Song Dynasty, demonstrating the abundant social wealth at that time and the unique history of the port in Quanzhou which relied on an agricultural empire. The Stone Statue of Lao Tze showed the prevalence of Taoism, the diversity of folk beliefs, and the coexistence of Confucianism, Taoism and Buddhism in Quanzhou at that time. It also reflects the multiple and dynamic cultures of Quanzhou as a world maritime trade center, as well as the prosperity and achievements of the port.

老君岩造像高 5.63 米，厚 6.85 米，宽 8.01 米，是中国现存年代最早、体量最大的古代道教石雕老君造像。（李芸生 摄）
The Statue of Lao Tze, the earliest extant and largest ancient Taoist stone sculpture of Lao Tze in China, is 5.63 meters high, 6.85 meters thick and 8.01 meters wide. (Photo by Li Yunsheng)

泉州的道教文化

道教是中国的本土宗教，源于古代的巫术、秦汉时的神仙方术。东汉末年，张道陵创立五斗米道，奉老子为教主，并将《老子》（又名《道德经》）列为经典，把“道”作为其最高、最根本的信仰，由此逐渐形成道教。道教逐渐形成以太上老君为信仰核心，以各路“神仙”系统作为信仰体系的中国本土宗教。

道教在泉州传播的历史十分悠久。泉州的道教信仰始于晋朝，盛于唐宋，明清以后逐渐走向世俗化与民间化。漫长的历史演变中，道教在泉州留下了丰富的历史遗迹与文化遗产。

Taoist Culture in Quanzhou

Taoism, an indigenous Chinese religion, originated from ancient sorcery and immortal arts in the Qin (221 B.C.—207 B.C.) and Han (206 B.C.—220 A.D.) Dynasties. At the end of Eastern Han Dynasty (25—220), Zhang Daoling established the religion called Way of the Five Pecks of Rice, which regarded Lao Tze as the founder, *Lao Tze* (also named *Tao Te Ching*, *Daodejing*, *Dao De Jing*, or *Daode Jing*) as its classic, and Tao (Dao) as its highest and most fundamental belief. Therefore, Taoism was gradually formed. Taoism gradually became an indigenous religion in China with Taishang Laojun (namely Lao Tze) as its main god, supplemented with other Chinese gods.

Taoism in Quanzhou boasts a rich history of centuries. The belief began in the Jin Dynasty (266—420), prospered in the Tang and Song Dynasties, and gradually became secularized and popular after the Ming and Qing Dynasties. In the long history of its evolution, Quanzhou preserves abundant relics and cultural heritage from its Taoist past.

西晋太康年间，泉州城区修建了白云庙（即元妙观的前身），这也成为泉州最早的道教宫观。（黄善哲 摄）

Baiyun Temple (formerly Yuanmiao Temple), built in the urban area of Quanzhou between 280 and 289 of the Western Jin Dynasty, is the earliest Taoist temple in Quanzhou. (Photo by Huang Shanzhe)

唐代崇奉道教，老子被尊封为“玄元皇帝”，道教得到地方官员的倡导与扶持。一批道教宫观得以在泉州修建，较著者有城西南的金粟崇真观、行春门外的紫极宫和清源山的紫泽洞。五代时，陈洪进于惠安兴建奉先观。这一时期，泉州晋江还出了个著名的道教学者谭峭，其著有《化书》六卷一百一十篇。《化书》作为道教的重要经典之一，被收入《道藏》中。

宋代，随着国家政治中心南移，尤其是泉州市舶司的设立使泉州有了较为完备的海外贸易管理机构，这为泉州港的进一步崛起奠定了制度性保障。这一时期，泉州兴建及重修了大批道教宫观，如：天庆观、广孝观、净真观、玉虚宫、玉华宫、柏庭观、碧虚观、真君宫、顺济宫、慈济宫、东岳行宫、城隍庙、法石真武行宫，清源山纯阳洞、北斗殿和真君殿，惠安崇真观，安溪通元观，南安三清宫，永春圣祖宫，德化崇道宫等。与此同时，泉州也涌现一批著名的道士，如北宋同安白礁（今漳州台商投资区白礁村）的吴夲、南安高镇山的詹道人、惠安龙泉的洪圣保、南安乌石山的徐道、天庆观道士林虚极，南宋清源山的裴道人、安溪月峰岩的崔道人、晋江金鞍山的赵永嘉、法石院的碧桃道人、德化石牛山的张慈观和陈朗等。此外，地方官员还亲自主持或参与九日山祈风与法石真武庙祭海等活动。

泉州东岳行宫与南少林寺仅一墙之隔。（李芸生 摄）
Dongyue Palace and Southern Shaolin Temple in Quanzhou are neighbors. (Photo by Li Yunsheng)

During the Tang Dynasty, Taoism was worshipped and Lao Tze was honored with the title "Emperor Xuanyuan". Local officials actively supported Taoism, leading to the construction of numerous Taoist temples across the city. Among them are Jinsu Chongzhen Temple in the southwest of Quanzhou, Ziji Palace outside Xingchun Gate and Zize Cave (Zize Temple) on Qingyuan Mountain. During the period of the Five Dynasties, Chen Hongjin built Fengxian Temple in Hui'an County. At the same time, Tan Qiao, a famous Taoist scholar from Jinjiang in Quanzhou, wrote *Of Transformation*, containing a total of 6 volumes and 110 chapters. The book has been included in *Tao-tsang* (or *Taoist Canon*) as an essential Taoist classics.In the Song Dynasty, as China's political center moved to the south, especially the establishment of the Maritime Trade Office in Quanzhou, a relatively complete foreign trade management institution was set in Quanzhou, which laid institutional guarantees for the further rise of Quanzhou Port.

During this period, Quanzhou witnessed the construction and renovation of numerous Taoist temples and palaces, including Tianqing Temple, Guangxiao Temple, Jingzhen Temple, Yuxu Palace, Yuhua Palace, Baiting Temple, Bixu Temple, Zhenjun Palace, Shunji Palace, Ciji Palace, Dongyue Palace, Town God's Temple, Fashi Zhenwu Palace, Chunyang Cave (Chunyang Temple) on Qingyuan Mountain, Beidou Hall, Zhenjun Hall, Chongzhen Temple in Hui'an, Tongyuan Temple in Anxi, Sanqing Palace in Nan'an, Shengzu Palace in Yongchun, Chongdao Palace in Dehua, etc. At the same time, many famous Taoists appeared, such as Wu Tao in Baijiao in Tong'an (today's Baijiao Village in Zhangzhou Taiwanese Investment Zone), Taoist Zhan of Gaozhen Mountain in Nan'an, Hong Shengbao of Longquan in Hui'an, Xu Dao of Wushi Mountain in Nan'an and Lin Xuji of Tianqing Temple in the Northern Song Dynasty, and Taoist Pei of Qingyuan Mountain, Taoist Cui of Yuefeng Rock in Anxi, Zhao Yongjia of Jin'an Mountain in Jinjiang, Taoist Bitao of Fashi Temple, Zhang Ciguan and Chen Lang of Shiniu Mountain in Dehua in the Southern Song Dynasty. In addition, local officials presided over or participated in praying ceremonies such as wind praying ceremonies on Jiuri Mountain and sacrificial rituals for the sea god in Fashi Zhenwu Temple.

供奉保生大帝吴夲的白礁慈济宫。（蔡文原 摄）
Baijiao Ciji Palace deifies Wu Tao, God Baosheng (the God of Medicine). (Photo by Cai Wenyuan)

元代,朝廷对道教全真派、正一派也给予一定的支持,永春修建了三清观,南安建有吴真人祠。明清两朝,国家设置道官检束天下道士,一方面对道教活动加以限制,一方面也对道教加以利用,如将泉州通淮关岳庙、泉州府城隍庙列为春秋祭祀的场所,在施琅收复台湾后晋封妈祖为"天后"等。此时,儒、道、释进一步合流,许多宫庙出现佛道并祀的情况,道教进一步民间化。同时,道教文化也随着本地商人的海外商贸活动足迹向东南亚和世界各地传播。

道教文化也影响到泉州地名的变迁,如在清源山上的清源洞(又名纯阳洞)列清源山三十六洞岩之首,被称为"第一洞天"。南宋绍兴间裴道人到此修行,后坐化于清源洞,洞外有"蜕岩""羽化登仙""有仙则名"等摩崖题刻。裴道人在"羽化"前,时常到西街一条巷口卖草药,后来人们也将该巷称为"裴巷"。

泉郡富美宫作为闽台两地的"王爷总馆",是"王爷信俗和送王船"的重要传播源头,对闽台乃至东南亚地区的王爷信仰、送王船习俗产生了深远的影响。2020 年 12 月 17 日,我国与马来西亚联合申报的"送王船——有关人与海洋可持续联系的仪式及相关实践"被列入《人类非物质文化遗产代表作名录》。此外,泉州地方戏曲中的《八仙庆寿》《韩湘子得道》等曲目也与道教神仙有关。

清源山清源洞。(成冬冬 摄)

Qingyuan Cave of Qingyuan Mountain. (Photo by Cheng Dongdong)

During the Yuan Dynasty, the imperial court also supported Quanzhen School and Zhengyi School of Taoism, building Sanqing Palace in Yongchun and Wu Zhenren (Immortal Wu) Temple in Nan'an. During the Ming and Qing Dynasties, the governments appointed Taoist officials to regulate Taoist priests across the country, which was to both restrict Taoist activities and to make use of Taoism, such as designating Tonghuai Guanyue Temple and Town God's Temple in Quanzhou as ritual sites in spring and fall and conferring the title "Heavenly Empress" to Mazu after Shi Lang reunified Taiwan. During this period, Confucianism, Taoism and Buddhism integrated further and, in many temples, both Buddhas and Taoist Gods were worshiped. Gradually Taoism became more secular. Meanwhile, Taoist culture also spread to Southeast Asia and elsewhere in the world along with overseas trade activities of the merchants in Quanzhou.

Taoist culture also influenced the changes of place names in Quanzhou. For example, Qingyuan Cave (also Chunyang Cave), known as "The First Fairyland", tops the 36 caves on Qingyuan Mountain. During 1131 and 1162 of the Southern Song Dynasty, Taoist Pei came here to practice Taoism and finally passed away in Qingyuan Cave. Outside the cave are rock inscriptions with Tui Yan (rock where Taoists ascend to immortality), Yu Hua Deng Xian (ascending to heaven and becoming immortals), and You Xian Ze Ming (a place will become famous when immortals emerge from here). Before Taoist Pei's ascension, he often sold herbal medicine at the mouth of an alley in West Street. Therefore, the locals named the alley "Pei Alley".

Fumei Palace, the center of the Wangye belief for Fujian and Taiwan, is an important source of the Wangye Faith and Wangchuan Ceremony. It has a profound influence on the Wangye Faith and Wangchuan Ceremony in Fujian, Taiwan, and Southeast Asia. On December 17, 2020, the project "Wangchuan Ceremony, Rituals and Related Practices for Maintaining the Sustainable Connection Between Man and the Ocean", nominated by China together with Malaysia, was listed on the Representative List of the Intangible Cultural Heritage of Humanity. In addition, Quanzhou's operas like *The Eight Immortals Celebrate the Birthday of God of Longevity* and *Han Xiangzi Ascending to Immortality* are also related to Taoist immortals and deities.

泉州的“送王船”仪式。（苏德辉　摄）

Wangchuan Ceremony in Quanzhou. (Photo by Su Dehui)

大道至简：老子天下第一

老君岩所在的清源山是泉州重要的道教活动场所，留存有众多的道教史迹。清源山作为泉州的主山，位于泉州古城的北面，也称北山，属于戴云山余脉。清源山具有沿海花岗岩山岳的典型特征，整个地形除了南面与泉州市区平原接壤外，大部分是山地丘陵，如同巨大的屏障，拱卫着泉州城。

泉州老君岩造像高 5.63 米，宽 8.01 米，厚 6.85 米。造像择址山林，坐北朝南，背屏青山，面向古城，巍然端坐，一派安详自得的样子，展现了浑然天成的美学。正如乾隆版《泉州府志》中所提到的："石像天成，好事者为略施雕琢。"明代林胤昌在《清源洞游记》中也提到老君气象如虎："独老君岿然露顶而坐，俯视鲤城，掀髯睁眼，凛有生气。昔夫子见老子以为犹龙，而兹像余见以为犹虎也。"

清源山是国家级风景名胜区、首批国家自然与文化双遗产、国家 5A 级旅游景区。（陈英杰 摄）
Qingyuan Mountain is a national-level scenic spot, on the first batch of both national natural and cultural heritages, and also a national 5A-level scenic spot. (Photo by Chen Yingjie)

Simplicity as the Ultimate Sophistication: Lao Tze, the Wisest

Qingyuan Mountain, where the Statue of Lao Tze is located, holds immense importance in Quanzhou's Taoist heritage. As the largest mountain in Quanzhou, Qingyuan Mountain is located in the north of Quanzhou City, so it is also known as "Northern Mountain", and belongs to the Daiyun Range. Qingyuan Mountain has the typical characteristics of coastal granitic mountains, with most of its terrain composed of mountains and hills but the south adjoining the plain of the urban area of Quanzhou, like a huge protecting screen wall guarding the city.

The Statue of Lao Tze is 5.63 meters high, 8.01 meters wide and 6.85 meters thick. Facing south, it is situated in a forest, with green mountains behind it and Quanzhou in its front. It sits majestically, exuding a calm and contented atmosphere. The whole statue looks like a huge one carved by nature. As mentioned in the Qianlong edition of *Local Chronicles of Quanzhou Prefecture*, "The stone statue was naturally formed and the carver only made minor modifications." Lin Yinchang also mentioned it in *Qingyuan Cave Travelogue* in the Ming Dynasty that the Statue of Lao Tze had the demeanor of a tiger: "The Statue of Lao Tze sits solemnly, with the sky above its head. It gazes down upon the ancient city of Quanzhou. With eyes wide open and beard flying, it seems almost alive. Confucius once regarded Lao Tze as a dragon, but I think it is a tiger."

泉州老君岩造像雕刻于宋代，系利用一块露出地面的天然花岗岩石雕琢而成。（刘宝生 摄）
The Statue of Lao Tze in Quanzhou was carved out of a naturally exposed granite in the Song Dynasty. (Photo by Liu Baosheng)

老君即太上老君，姓李，名耳，号聃，又号老子，是春秋末期卓越的思想家，也是道家学派创始人，其代表作《老子》作为道教的经典，内容涵盖哲学、政治学、伦理学等诸多学科，是影响深远的中国古代思想著作。老子的主要思想是“无为而治”，讲究一切顺其自然，强调物极必反，体现了古代中国人的世界观和人生观。道教于东汉末年由张道陵创立，尊奉老子为道教教主并衍化为道教“三清”之一的“太清道德天尊”。

清源山老君造像姿态从容，脸含微笑，双目平视，双耳垂肩，鼻梁高突，苍髯飘洒，左手按膝，右手凭几，充分展示了老子的仙风道骨与超凡脱俗。老君屈足着靴，身穿对衽道袍席地凭几倾坐，衣褶线条流畅分明，体现了“大道至简”的宋人风雅美学，正如《道德经》中所记：“大音希声，大象无形，道隐无名。”

Lao Jun, the "Highest Elder Lord", Li Er by personal name and Dan and Lao Tze by literary names, is an eminent thinker during the late Spring and Autumn Period (770 B.C.—476 B.C.) and the founder of the Taoist school of thought. His masterpiece *Lao Tze* (or *Tao Te Ching*) serves as a Taoist classic covering philosophy, politics, ethics, and many other disciplines. It is an ancient Chinese work of thought with profound influence. Lao Tze's main idea is "ruling through non-action", advocating following nature and emphasizing that things will develop in their opposite directions when they become extreme, which reflects the ancient Chinese worldview and philosophy of life. Taoism was established by Zhang Daoling at the end of the Eastern Han Dynasty, regarding Lao Tze as the founder, who later became one of the "Three Pure Ones", namely "Taiqing Daode Tianzun" (The Heavenly Lord of Tao and Virtue).

The Statue of Lao Tze in Qingyuan Mountain appears calm and serene, with a smile and eyes gazing straight ahead. Its ears reach its shoulder, nose ridge protruding high and grey beard hanging freely. Its left hand rests on its knee while the right hand on a table, fully displaying Lao Tze's immortal spirit and transcendence of the mundane. It sits with its legs bended, wearing boots, clad in a Taoist robe and sitting on the ground leaning against a table. The neat and distinct folds of the clothing embody the aesthetic concept "simplicity as the ultimate sophistication" in the Song Dynasty. As recorded in *Tao Te Ching*, "Great music has the faintest notes, the great form is without shape and Tao is hidden and nameless."

老君岩造像细部及案几云纹图案。（成冬冬 摄）
The details of the Statue of Lao Tze and cloud patterns on the table. (Photo by Cheng Dongdong)

《道德经》中还写道：“五色令人目盲，五音令人耳聋。”缤纷的色彩，使人眼花缭乱；嘈杂的声音，使人听觉失灵。这句话在老君岩造像上也得到体现，正所谓“藏目”“掩耳”。

就其工艺特点而言，老君岩造像整体雕工精细，形态生动，须眉分明，额纹、衣褶清晰，头、额、眼、鬓、须雕刻夸张而不失其意，庄重中又彰显灵动，简约中深蕴独特匠心，极具神韵，益显道家“天人合一、道法自然”的庄严意境。

明代御史季本曾有诗句赞老君岩造像曰：“同游共宴坐，谈道各知雄。冥探谢侈哆，妙契以参同。出门未数武，翼然见新宫。内有老子像，炳焕生龙光。刻画渺难察，奇巧疑天工。吾闻太上数，当在关西东。如何闽海渺，亦留现世踪。”由此可知在老君岩造像之上曾有宫庙建筑存在。这也从 1990 年底于老君岩周边出土的带靴楔栌斗、带靴楔交互斗、绰幕方残件、券门楔石等建筑构件得到了印证，而这些石构件又与泉州开元寺东西塔、六胜塔等建筑构件相似。

“老子天下第一”石刻。（刘宝生 摄）
The stone inscription "Lao Tze Tianxia Diyi" (Lao Tze, the Wisest). (Photo by Liu Baosheng)

According to *Tao Te Ching*, "The five colours dim one's eyes and the five sounds dull one's ears", which can be seen in the Statue of Lao Tze through its covered eyes and ears.

In terms of the craftsmanship, the Statue of Lao Tze was carved exquisitely as a whole with vivid posture, distinct eyebrows and beard, clear forehead wrinkles and folds of clothes. The carvings of the head, forehead, eyes, beard, and mustache are exaggerated but well fitting, solemn yet spirited, and simple yet unique. These features are endowed with charm, manifesting the Taoist spirit "man is an integral part of nature and Tao operates naturally".

The censor Ji Ben in the Ming Dynasty once wrote an poem to praise the statue. The poem shows that there might be a temple built for the sculpture, which can be confirmed by the architectural components unearthed around the statue in late 1990, including cap blocks with shoe-patterned, wedges, connection blocks with shoe-patterned wedges, broken tiebeams, capstones of arched doors and other building components. These stone components are similar to those of the East Pagoda and the West Pagoda of Kaiyuan Temple and Liusheng Pagoda.

老君岩周边出土的石构件。（成冬冬 摄）
The stone components unearthed around the Statue of Lao Tze. (Photo by Cheng Dongdong)

关于老君岩的雕刻时间，有唐代说、北宋说、宋代说、南宋嘉定元年（1208）说、南宋淳祐以后说、元代说等数种。据明代何乔远《闽书》所载，当在宋代便已雕成："羽仙岩，在罗山、武山之下。宋罗山下，有北斗岩；武山下，有真君殿，朱文公尝游焉，今曰老君岩。盖石镌李老君须髯宴坐像，高十余尺，不知何年。宋淳祐不载，必淳祐以后镌也。"从这段描述也再次印证宋代老君岩造像之上曾盖有祠殿，而且朱熹曾到此游览。

老君岩造像作为泉州海外贸易兴盛而带来地方经济繁荣的产物，显示了当时泉州道教得到相当程度的发展、本土文化得到广泛的认同，并向世人展示了源远流长的中华传统文化的价值和生命力。

About the time when the Statue of Lao Tze was carved, there are multiple assumptions, including the Tang Dynasty, the Northern Song Dynasty, the Song Dynasty, the 1st year of Jiading Period (1208) of the Southern Song Dynasty, post-Chunyou Period (1241—1252) of the Southern Song Dynasty, and the Yuan Dynasty. According to *The Book of Min* by He Qiaoyuan in the Ming Dynasty, the statue should have been carved in the Song Dynasty, "Yuxian Rock, at the foot of Luoshan Hill and Wushan Hill; Beidou Rock, at the foot of Luoshan Hill in the Song Dynasty; now I see the Statue of Lao Tze in Zhenjun Hall, at the foot of Wushan Hill, which Zhu Xi once visited. It is a carved stone image of Lao Tze sitting quietly with beard hanging, which is over 3 meters high. I don't know when it was carved. If there is no record during Chunyou Period of the Song Dynasty, it must be carved after that." Once again, these words confirm that there was a temple for the sculpture in the Song Dynasty, and Zhu Xi visited it.

The Statue of Lao Tze, as a product of the local economic prosperity brought by the flourishing overseas trade in Quanzhou, demonstrates that Taoism had developed to a considerable degree and the native culture was widely accepted at that time, showing the value and vitality of long-lasting traditional Chinese culture to the world.

番商胡贾，天方来朝——伊斯兰教圣墓、清净寺

Islamic Tombs and Qingjing Mosque: Foreign Merchants Spurred Cultural Blending

先贤的墓地

The Tombs of Two Sages

被淡忘的圣友寺与被记住的清净寺

Shengyou Mosque and Qingjing Mosque: the Lost and the Preserved

泉州穆斯林的节庆与礼俗

The Festivals, Etiquette and Customs of Muslims in Quanzhou

灵山伊斯兰教圣墓为伊斯兰世界现存最古老、最完好的圣迹之一，是全国重点文物保护单位。（刘宝生 摄）

As one of the oldest and best-preserved holy remains in the Islamic world, Lingshan Islamic Tombs are a national key cultural relics protection unit. (Photo by Liu Baosheng)

伊斯兰教作为世界性宗教之一，早在公元 7 世纪就随着穆斯林传播到中国，泉州则是伊斯兰教最早传入中国的地区之一。唐武德年间，伊斯兰教创始人穆罕默德派遣门徒四人来华传教，其中三贤、四贤传教泉州，卒后葬于清源山东翼的灵山。沿着先贤的足迹，众多阿拉伯人、波斯人在海上丝绸之路繁盛时期来到泉州，至元代时人数一度达到高峰。他们经商、传教、游历，当中许多人定居泉州，聚族而居、繁衍后代。他们在此建造清真寺，置墓葬区，为世界留下了伊斯兰文化的重要历史遗产。

As one of the world's major religions, Islam spread to China as early as the 7th century with the arrival of Muslims. Quanzhou is one of the earliest regions where Islam reached in China. During 618 and 626 of the Tang Dynasty, the Islamic prophet Muhammad sent four disciples to preach in China. Among them, two preached in Quanzhou. After their deaths, they were buried on Lingshan Hill. Following the path of the sages, many Arabs and Persians came to Quanzhou during the prosperous period of the Maritime Silk Road, reaching its peak in the Yuan Dynasty. They engaged in trade, preaching, and traveling, with many of them settling in Quanzhou, living together to form communities, producing offspring, and leaving behind an important historical heritage of Islamic culture by building mosques and establishing burial areas here.

泉州清净寺始建于北宋大中祥符二年（1009），是阿拉伯穆斯林在中国创建的现存最古老的伊斯兰教寺。（陈英杰 摄）

Qingjing Mosque was first built in 1009 of the Northern Song Dynasty. It is the oldest extant Islamic mosque built by Arab Muslims in China. (Photo by Chen Yingjie)

先贤的墓地

据明代史学家何乔远所著《闽书》记载，相传在唐武德年间穆罕默德门徒四人来华，一贤传教广州；二贤传教扬州；三贤、四贤传教泉州，二人卒后葬于东门外灵山南麓，故又称“三贤四贤”墓。因两位先贤深受穆斯林敬重，其入土安眠之地被称为“圣墓”。

The Tombs of Two Sages

According to *The Book of Min*, written by He Qiaoyuan, a historian in the Ming Dynasty, during 618 and 626 of the Tang Dynasty, four followers of the prophet Muhammad came to China as missionaries. One preached in Guangzhou, one in Yangzhou, and the other two settled down in Quanzhou. After the latter two passed away, they were buried at the southern foot of Lingshan Hill outside the East Gate of Quanzhou City. Highly respected by Muslims, their tombs were then named "Holy Tombs".

现存灵山圣墓主体为元至治二年（1322）修缮后的遗存。（成冬冬 摄）
The existing remains of Lingshan Islamic Tombs' main structure were restored in 1322 of the Yuan Dynasty. (Photo by Cheng Dongdong)

按照伊斯兰教墓葬风俗，墓葬形式应为头北足南，侧身面向西，即伊斯兰教圣地麦加的方向，墓前有可供穆斯林瞻礼时举行必要仪式的旷地。灵山圣墓即按照此风俗建造。灵山圣墓坐北面南，依山而筑，主体布局由一圈半月形的回廊环抱两座石墓。石墓以花岗岩雕成，并列排布，是泉州典型的穆斯林石墓形式。

According to the burial custom of Islam, the body should be placed with the face turning towards the west, which is the direction of Mecca, while the head laid down towards the north and the feet towards the south. In front of tombs is an open area for Muslims to perform necessary rituals when paying respects. The main structure of Lingshan Ismalic Tombs faces the south, built along the mountain's slope. A winding corridor in the shape of a crescent moon surrounds the two tombs. Both tombs were carved out of granite and arranged in a row, typical of Muslim stone tombs in Quanzhou.

三贤四贤墓石墓盖。（成冬冬 摄）
The stone tomb caps of the two sages. (Photo by Cheng Dongdong)

两座东西并列的花岗岩石雕琢而成的伊斯兰教墓盖石，墓石分三层，逐层内收。第一层即底座，浮雕莲瓣纹一圈；中层作素面；第三层为横截面呈圆拱状的顶盖石。上有墓亭，为仿木石构，四圆柱，歇山顶。

墓东、西、北三面依山筑有石构回廊拱护，石廊为仿木梁柱结构，九开间，以石雕为础、柱、斗、梁、枋等构件。廊柱中保留有数根柱体上下作蜷缩状的梭柱，也就是柱身中段粗、首尾细。据考古学家研究，这是南朝至唐代流行的做法。另外在柱上以方形大斗承托卷云纹的雀替状支撑构件，这也与清净寺门楼的雀替状构件雕饰相近。

The two side-by-side tomb caps are made of granite and each has three layers, like pyramids. The bottom layer was carved with lotus petal patterns, the central layer was unadorned, and the top layer is the cap stone with a vault-shaped section. Above the tombs stands a stone tomb pavilion in imitation of timber-framed construction, with four round pillars and a saddle roof.

Stone corridors were built against hills along the east, west, and north sides to protect the tombs. The nine-*chien* stone corridors are in imitation of wooden beam and column structures, using carved stones as building components, such as the base, pillars, bracket sets, beams, tiebeams and others. Some of the pillars are shuttle-shaped, which are thicker in the middle and thinner at both ends. According to archaeologists, this is a common practice from the Southern Dynasty (420—589) to the Tang Dynasty. In addition, the pillars have square brackets to hold sparrow like braces supporting components with curling cloud patterns, like the decorations on the gatehouse of Qingjing Mosque.

石构墓廊拱护着三贤四贤墓。（成冬冬 摄）
The stone-constructed corridors arched to protect the tombs of the two sages. (Photo by Cheng Dongdong)

现在墓廊内及挡墙壁还保存着自元代以来的七通碑刻，墓廊正中为元至治二年（1322）修缮时立的《重修圣墓碑》。碑文为阿拉伯文，记述三贤、四贤事略以及元代泉州穆斯林重新修缮圣墓的经过。墓廊中另一方重要的石刻为《郑和行香碑》，这是一方记录明永乐十五年（1417）郑和在第五次下西洋路经泉州，来此祭拜先贤、行香祈求庇佑的汉文石碑。此外，还有清康熙五十三年（1714），陈有功、陈美共同修缮圣墓留下的碑记；嘉庆二十三年（1818），署福建全省督军门、漳州总镇马建纪修缮圣墓，再建墓亭留下的碑记；同治十年（1871），福建提督江长贵修缮圣墓留下的碑记。挡墙嵌有乾隆辛未年（1751）董事夏必第修缮圣墓留下的碑记，以及乾隆四十八年（1783）举人郭拔萃修缮圣墓留下的碑记。这些碑记成为研究中国伊斯兰教和灵山圣墓历史的重要文物。

Seven stone steles dating back to the Yuan Dynasty have been preserved in the corridors and tomb enclosure walls. In the middle of the corridor stands the inscription *Stele for the Reconstruction of the Islamic Tombs* erected when the tombs were repaired in 1322 of the Yuan Dynasty. The inscription is in Arabic, recording the histories of the two sages settling in Quanzhou and the process of renovating the tombs by Quanzhou Muslims during the Yuan Dynasty. Another important stele, *Stele of Zheng He's Pilgrimage*, is in Chinese, recording that Zheng He passed by Quanzhou on his 5th voyage and came to worship the sages and pray for blessings in 1417 of the Ming Dynasty. There are also steles about when people repaired the tombs during the Qing Dynasty, including those about Chen Yougong and Chen Mei repairing the tombs in 1714, Ma Jianji, a military commander of Fujian Province repairing the tombs and rebuilding the pavilion in 1818, and Jiang Changgui, a military governor of Fujian Province, repairing the tombs in 1871. The tomb enclosure walls were inlaid with the inscriptions made when director Xia Bidi repaired the tombs in 1751, and Guo Bacui, an eminent scholar repaired the tombs in 1783. These steles are important relics for researching Islam in China and the history of Lingshan Islamic Tombs.

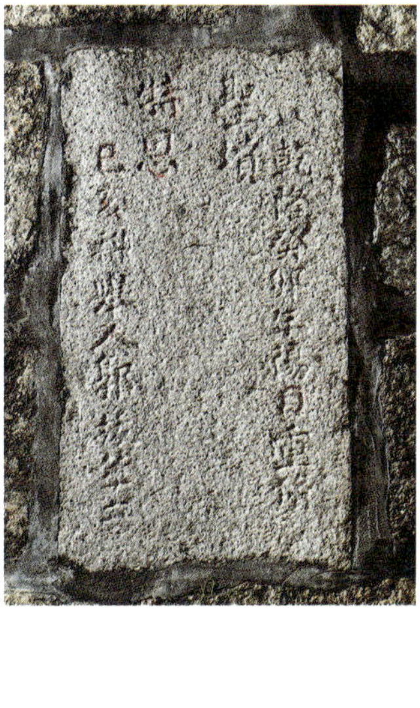

《重修圣墓碑》《郑和行香碑》及墓廊系列碑刻。（成冬冬 摄）

Stele for the Reconstruction of the Islamic Tombs, *Stele of Zheng He's Pilgrimage*, and other steles in the corridor of the tombs of two sages. (Photo by Cheng Dongdong)

在圣墓前有一块自然天成的风动石，上面题写着“碧玉毬”与“天然机妙”等文字。“碧玉毬”是明代泉州太守周道光所题，“天然机妙”为清代署福建全省督军门马建纪所题。

圣墓东南部的山麓地带为 14 世纪以来历代沿用的一片穆斯林公墓，其中最为有名的是陈埭丁氏的墓葬区。这一片穆斯林公墓墓葬既有汉人墓葬的形制，同时保留着阿拉伯塔式石墓盖。700 多年前，丁氏先民沿着“海上丝绸之路”自阿拉伯国家而来，凭借着善于经商的能力，将伊斯兰文化与汉文化相互交融与结合，形成了一个汉文化与伊斯兰文化相互交织的独特群体——丁氏回族。据丁氏族谱记载：“吾族丁氏，肇基于始祖节斋公，由姑苏行贾入泉，居于桐城之文山里，递传三世，至硕德公，徙居陈江，子孙繁衍，文物蔚起。”由此可知丁氏家族的祖先丁谨（号节斋），于宋末从苏州来泉州经商。元朝至正末，三世丁夔携子丁善移居陈埭，并定居繁衍至今。

圣墓前的风动石为泉州八景中的“玉毬风动”。（刘宝生 摄）
The wind-moving stone in front of the Islamic Tombs is known as "Jade Ball Moving with Wind", one of the eight scenic spots in Quanzhou. (Photo by Liu Baosheng)

In front of the tombs is a naturally formed stone called Fengdong Stone, inscribed with the Chinese characters "Biyuqiu" (meaning its color and shape like a jade ball) and "Tianran Jimiao" (meaning natural and delicate) respectively by Quanzhou Prefect Zhou Daoguang in the Ming Dynasty and the provincial military commander Ma Jianji in the Qing Dynasty.

To the southeast of the Islamic Tombs, at the foot of the mountain there is an area having been used as a Muslim cemetery for generations since the 14th century, notably the burial ground of Ding family of Chendai Town. This Muslim cemetery retains Arabic stone tomb covers as well as the burial designs of Han people. Over 700 years ago, their ancestors arrived here via the Maritime Silk Road from Arab countries. With excellent business skills, they blended Islamic and Chinese cultures, forming a unique Hui ethnic group. The Ding's genealogy records, "Our ancestor Lord Jiezhai traveled from Suzhou to Quanzhou for trade, living in Wenshanli Village, Quanzhou City. Three generations later, Lord Shuode led them to move to Chendai, and their descendants flourished with wealth and learning." So, Ding Jin (Jiezhai by literary name) came to Quanzhou from Suzhou for business in the late Song Dynasty. At the end of the Zhizheng Period (1341—1368) of the Yuan Dynasty, Ding Kui, Ding Jin's grandson, and his son Ding Shan settled down in Chendai where they have lived and thrived to this day.

位于圣墓东南方的陈埭丁氏墓葬区。（成冬冬 摄）
The burial area of the Ding family of Chendai Town to the southeast of the Islamic Tombs. (Photo by Cheng Dongdong)

伊斯兰教圣墓是宋元时期穆斯林商人及其族群在泉州活动的见证。从墓盖石整体造型上来看符合伊斯兰文化特征，但最下层环刻的莲瓣纹则是中国文化中常用的装饰。此外，坐北面南、依山而筑的选址符合中国传统建筑选址观念。这些特征显示出海洋贸易带来的外来文化与本土文化的交往与融合。

时至今日，伊斯兰教圣墓依然吸引众多海内外穆斯林前来瞻仰、朝拜。每逢伊斯兰重要节日，多有穆斯林来此拜谒先贤、念诵《古兰经》、举行游坟活动等，这也是泉州穆斯林恪守不渝的风俗习惯。

The Islamic tombs bear a testimony to the activities of Muslim merchants and their communities in Quanzhou during the Song and Yuan Dynasties. The overall design of the stone tomb caps conforms to the characteristics of Islamic culture, while the lotus petal pattern carved in the lower layer is a common decoration in Chinese culture. In addition, the fact that the tombs face the south and were built along the hillside conforms to the traditional Chinese concept of selecting building sites. These characteristics demonstrate the interaction and blending between foreign and local cultures facilitated by maritime trade.

Today, Lingshan Islamic Tombs are still attracting plenty of Muslim pilgrims from both China and abroad to come to worship and pay their respects. On important Islamic holidays, many Muslims come here to pay homage to the two sages, recite *Quran*, and hold tomb-sweeping activities, which has been an unwavering custom for Quanzhou Muslims.

穆斯林到圣墓拜谒先贤、举行游坟活动。（刘宝生 摄）
Muslims are visiting the Islamic Tombs to pay respects to the two sages and holding tomb-sweeping activities. (Photo by Liu Baosheng)

被淡忘的圣友寺与被记住的清净寺

涂门街是泉州古城内文化遗存最为丰富的街区之一，从西往东分别坐落着代表儒家文化的泉州府文庙、代表伊斯兰文化的清净寺，同时还有锡兰王子后裔的旧居、民间信仰的重要代表——关岳庙。宋元时期，跨越重洋来泉州经商的波斯（今伊朗）、阿拉伯等地穆斯林在此定居，繁盛时修建的清真寺多达六七座，其中以清净寺最为著名。清净寺位于泉州古城南部商业性城区，历代穆斯林围绕清净寺聚族而居，形成独特的穆斯林社区。

千年以来，各种宗教信仰和谐共处于涂门街，见证着泉州文化的包容融合与多元性。（许兆恺 摄）

Over a thousand years, the harmonious coexistence of the various religious beliefs on Tumen Street is a witness to the inclusiveness, integration, and diversity of the cultures in Quanzhou. (Photo by Xu Zhaokai)

Shengyou Mosque and Qingjing Mosque: the Lost and the Preserved

Tumen Street is one of the most culturally rich districts in ancient Quanzhou. From west to east are located Quanzhou Confucian Temple representing Confucian culture, Qingjing Mosque symbolizing Islamic culture, the former residence of Sri Lankan prince's descendants, and Guanyue Temple, an important representative of folk beliefs. The Song and Yuan Dynasties witnessed that a great many Muslims from Persia (Iran nowadays), Arabia, and other places came to Quanzhou for business and settled here, and built as many as six or seven mosques. Among them, Qingjing Mosque is the most famous. Located in the southern commercial district of Quanzhou, Qingjing Mosque has acted as the center for the Muslims in Quanzhou throughout the generations, forming a distinctive Muslim community.

泉州清净寺，又名“圣友寺”（阿拉伯语译为“艾苏哈卜寺”），始建于北宋大中祥符二年（1009）。元至大三年（1310），由来自波斯设拉子城的朝觐者艾哈迈德·本·穆罕默德·古德斯出资修缮。作为我国现存最古老的伊斯兰教寺院之一，清净寺现有重要遗存包括石构门楼、望月台、奉天坛、明善堂等，呈现鲜明的西亚伊斯兰教寺院特征。

清净寺的门楼为伊斯兰风格建筑，通高 12.3 米，基宽 6.6 米，全部采用加工平整的花岗岩石和辉绿岩石砌筑。尖拱门上方有一列阿拉伯文《古兰经》石刻：“除真主外，绝无应受崇拜的，他是万能的，是至睿的。”门楼整体由三层四道高大相连的半穹顶或穹顶尖拱门组成。第一、二进门道外观均为尖拱形，顶部均为半穹顶，主体风格为伊斯兰穹顶式样，又融合了中国传统建筑中的藻井装饰风格。第三进门道顶部为穹顶，其南北两侧门洞尖拱下方的支撑构件类似中国传统建筑中的雀替。

清净寺门楼。（李祖耀 摄）
The Gatehouse of Qingjing Mosque. (Photo by Li Zuyao)

Qingjing Mosque in Quanzhou, also known as Shengyou Mosque (Masjid al-Ashab in Arabic), was built in 1009 of the Song Dynasty. In 1310 of the Yuan Dynasty, it was repaired by Ahmad Bin Muhammad Quds, a pilgrim from Shiraz, Persia (Iran nowadays). As one of the oldest surviving Islamic mosques in China, Qingjing Mosque has important remnants such as stone Gatehouse, Moon Watching Platform, Fengtian Altar, and Mingshan Hall showcasing distinct features of West Asian Islamic mosque architecture.

The Gatehouse of Qingjing Mosque showcases an Islamic style, 12.3 meters high and 6.6 meters wide at its base. It was constructed entirely with finely processed granites and diabase stones. Above the pointed arch of the Gatehouse was inscribed a verse from *Quran* in Arabic stating: "There is no god but Allah, and he is Almighty and All-Wise." The gatehouse comprises three layers of four tall connected semi-domes or domed pointed arches. The exterior appearance of both the first and second gateways feature pointed arches topped by semi-domes, exhibiting a dominant Islamic dome style integrated with elements of traditional Chinese architecture such as caisson ceilings. The third gateway has a full dome, while the supporting structure beneath its pointed arches on the north and south sides is similar to *queti* (sparrow brace), a traditional Chinese architectural component.

清净寺门楼穹顶。（成冬冬 摄）
The dome atop the Gatehouse of Qingjing Mosque. (Photo by Cheng Dongdong)

关于清净寺的修缮过程，在门楼北墙上有一段阿拉伯碑文，其译文是："此地人们的第一座礼拜寺，就是这座最古老、悠久、吉祥的礼拜寺，名称'艾苏哈卜寺'，建于回历400年（1009—1010）。300余年后，艾哈迈德·本·穆罕默德·古德斯，即设拉子著名的鲁克伯哈只，修复并更新了它，建筑高悬的穹顶，加阔了甬道，重修了高贵的寺门并翻新了窗户，于回历710年（1310—1311）竣工。"这段碑文明确记载了两个信息：一是这座清净寺始建于1009年，是泉州最早的礼拜寺；二是来自波斯设拉子的穆斯林于1310年重修了这座礼拜寺，所以清净寺在建筑风格上也受到了色拉子当地清真寺建筑的影响。

门楼屋顶为平台，四面环形建筑围成"回"字形垛子。南垛高1.4米，北垛高1.2米，左右嵌有两方阴刻"月""台"碑石，称"望月台"，是伊斯兰教斋月里阿訇登临望月、决定开斋日期的地方。

An Arabic inscription on the north wall of Qingjing Mosque's Gatehouse documenting the mosque's renovation process says, "The Masjid al-Ashab Mosque is the first, most ancient and auspicious mosque in Quanzhou, built in the 400th year of the Islamic calendar (1009—1010). Over 300 years later, Ahmad Bin Muhammad Jadis, a famous architect from Shiraz, repaired and renovated it. He raised the height of the dome, widened the corridor, restored the noble gate, renovated the windows, and completed the project in the 710th year of the Islamic calendar (1310—1311)." This inscription clearly records two pieces of information: first, Qingjing Mosque was built in 1009, making it the earliest mosque in Quanzhou; second, Muslim architects from Shiraz in Persia repaired the mosque in 1310, indicating that the architectural style of Qingjing Mosque was also influenced by local mosques in Shiraz.

The top of the Gatehouse is a platform surrounded by circular buildings in the form of the Chinese character " 回 ". The southern stack is 1.4 meters high while the northern one is 1.2 meters high. On the left and right sides stand two incised stone tablets inscribed with the characters "月 (moon)" and "台 (platform)", collectively known as Moon-Watching Platform. It serves for Akhund to climb up to observe the moon during Ramadan and determine the date for celebrating Eid al-Fitr.

清净寺门楼北墙阿拉伯文石刻。（成冬冬 摄）
Arabic inscriptions on the north wall of the gatehouse of Qingjing Mosque. (Photo by Cheng Dongdong)

奉天坛是穆斯林诵经礼拜之所。正门门楣部分雕刻阿拉伯文《古兰经》，大殿四壁均由花岗岩石砌成，巨大的窗户可以提高殿内采光效果。奉天坛西墙中部向西凸出部分为米哈拉布墙，指向伊斯兰教圣地麦加的方向，墙上开有七个尖拱形壁龛和六个门洞。龛中及尖拱顶石板均雕有阿拉伯文《古兰经》铭文。西墙壁龛（从南往北）第二龛的经文写道：“商业不能使他们疏忽而不纪念真主”，第六龛提到祈祷真主保佑到华贸易的航海者：“船舶在海中带着真主的恩惠而远行”，这也反映了经文与穆斯林的海上贸易活动有关。

1987 年 2 月，在国家文物局的指导下，福建省文管会组织考古队对奉天坛露天基址进行考古发掘，初步了解奉天坛内宋代至清代各个不同时期的文化堆积，以及奉天坛墙基 、磉墩的建筑结构。考古人员发现地下有宋元时期的建筑基址，判断应是清净寺始建时期的礼拜堂遗址及其附属建筑。

奉天坛旁边的古井，为建寺时挖掘，主要是供穆斯林前来举行礼拜之前汲水净身和信众平时日常生活饮用，井水至今仍清澈可用。

Fengtian Altar is a place for Muslims to pray and worship. The lintel of the main door is adorned with Arabic script from *Quran*. The main hall was constructed with granites and large windows can admit ample natural light. In the middle of the west wall of Fengtian Altar protrudes a recess known as Mihrab, indicating the direction of Mecca. The wall contains seven pointed arch niches and six doorways. The niches and tops of the pointed arches were inscribed with verses from *Quran* in Arabic script. The second niche from south to north mentions that commerce should not make them neglectful of the remembrance of Allah. The sixth niche mentions Allah's blessings on the voyagers of maritime trade, reflecting the linkage between the Quranic verses and the Muslims' maritime trading activities.

清净寺奉天坛米哈拉布墙。（成冬冬 摄）
The Mihrab of Fengtian Altar in Qingjing Mosque. (Photo by Cheng Dongdong)

In February 1987, guided by the National Cultural Heritage Administration, Fujian Cultural Heritage Management Commission organized an archaeological team to excavate the open-air site of Fengtian Altar. Through excavation they have gained a preliminary understanding of the cultural accumulations in different periods from the Song Dynasty to the Qing Dynasty, and studied the architectural structures of the altar's walls and foundations. They also discovered the building site from the Song and Yuan Dynasties, which is believed to be the site of worshiping hall and its annex in the early period of Qingjing Mosque.

The ancient well beside Fengtian Altar, dug during the mosque's construction, primarily serves for ablutions before Muslims said prayers, as well as for daily use. The water in the well is clear and drinkable to this day.

1987 年福建省文管会组织考古队对奉天坛露天基址进行了考古发掘。（成冬冬 摄）
In 1987, Fujian Cultural Heritage Management Commission organized an archaeological team to excavate the open-air site of Fengtian Altar. (Photo by Cheng Dongdong)

明善堂建于明隆庆元年（1567），为传统中式建筑。受伊斯兰教义中礼拜方向的要求，明善堂沿中轴线形成了东西朝向的布局方式，同时在内部构造上吸收了阿拉伯建筑的特点。正厅设置了领拜所用的圣龛，形成了具有浓郁民族宗教特色的建筑审美风格。

位于北侧围墙上的明永乐五年（1407）颁布的《敕谕》碑刻，是明成祖朱棣颁发保护伊斯兰教寺院的文告。碑文中有“今特授尔以敕谕护持，所在官员军民一应人等，毋得慢侮欺凌，敢有故违朕命慢侮欺凌者，以罪罪之”等句，要求各地官员、军民不得怠慢或欺凌穆斯林，违者治罪。

Mingshan Hall, constructed in 1567 of the Ming Dynasty, is a traditional Chinese building. In alignment with the Islamic doctrine of the direction of pray, its layout follows an east-west orientation along the central axis while also assimilating elements of Arab architecture within its internal structure. In the main hall a niche was set for the leading worshipper to face in prayer, forming the architectural aesthetics with distinct ethnic and religious identities.

The inscriptions on the north wall of Qingjing Mosque, carved in 1407 of the Ming Dynasty, comprises an imperial decree by Emperor Zhu Di (1360—1424) to protect Islamic mosques. It reads: "I hereby issue this decree of protection. All officials and soldiers must respect Muslims. Those who violate this decree shall be duly punished." The decree demands that the officials, armies, and common people across the country must not mistreat or bully Muslims.

明善堂是穆斯林进行较小规模礼拜的场所。（成冬冬 摄）
Mingshan Hall serves as a place for a modest scale of Muslim worship. (Photo by Cheng Dongdong)

位于门楼后的祝圣亭中立有两方碑刻。右侧的《重立清净寺碑》是由吴鉴撰于元至正十年（1350），属南门清净寺旧物。后因寺毁，该碑被移至涂门街清净寺。现碑为明正德二年（1507）重刻，碑中提到：“创兹寺于泉州之城南。今泉造礼拜寺，增为六、七。”左侧的《重修清净寺碑记》则是明万历三十七年（1609）李光缙所撰，记录了当时修缮清净寺的经过。碑文中提到：“楼峙文庙青龙之左角，有上下层，以西向为尊。”同时还提到太极、两仪、四象、八卦、十二月、二十四节气等中国传统概念，这也可以看出当时传统士大夫对于外来文化也会用中国文化加以解释。

In Zhusheng Pavilion behind the Gatehouse stand two stone inscriptions. The one on the right, titled *Re-establishment of Qingjing Mosque*, was written by Wu Jian in 1350 of the Yuan Dynasty and originally belonged to the former Qingjing Mosque at the South Gate. After the mosque was destroyed, it was moved to the current Qingjing Mosque on Tumen Street. The current stone inscription was re-carved in 1507. It says: "This mosque was established in the southern area of Quanzhou City. Now, there are six or seven mosques in Quanzhou." The inscription on the left titled *Repair of Qingjing Mosque*, written by Li Guangjin in 1609, documents the process of renovating Qingjing Mosque. The inscription mentions that: "The mosque's mihrab was a two-storey building facing west, which took up the left corner of the nearby Confucian Temple." It also mentions such traditional Chinese concepts as Taiji, *Liangyi* (namely Yin-Yang), *Sixiang* (Four symbols), Bagua, the twelve months, and the twenty-four solar terms. This indicates that Chinese scholars at that time would explain foreign cultures within their own cultural framework.

《重立清净寺碑》及《重修清净寺碑记》是中国伊斯兰寺院中可考的最早汉字碑记，对于研究早期阿拉伯与中国宗教文化交流史，伊斯兰教在中国东南沿海港口城市传播与清真寺的建置、组织机构等，都有珍贵的史料价值。（成冬冬 摄）

The steles of *Re-establishment of Qingjing Mosque* and *Repair of Qingjing Mosque* are the earliest Chinese inscriptions found in Islamic mosques in China. They have provided valuable historical materials for studying the early exchanges between Arabic and Chinese religions and cultures, the spread of Islam in southeast coastal Chinese cities, as well as the founding and organizations of Qingjing Mosque. (Photo by Cheng Dongdong)

清净寺是宋元时期泉州穆斯林商人及其族群的见证。这一群体是亚洲海洋贸易的主要参与者，也是宋元国家口岸城市多元社会结构的重要组成部分。清净寺的建筑风格及元素，体现了海洋贸易为泉州带来的人群汇聚和文化共存。这些多元文化元素极大地丰富了国家口岸城市的城市面貌和文化内涵。此外，清净寺修建之初位于泉州城外，随着12—13世纪外商聚居规模不断扩大以及城市向南扩张，也就将清净寺纳入城中。清净寺不仅是宋元泉州外商聚居区的珍贵遗存，也是商业性城区的重要地标，体现了宋元国家口岸城市独特的融合、发展过程。

清净寺的保护离不开泉州当地民众的执着与努力。正是这种发自内心的热爱与珍视，才使得清净寺建筑及文物得到很好的保存。通过清净寺所留存下来的空间格局与斑驳的砖石，以及透过石头上面镌刻的纹饰及铭文，使我们得以探知那段久远的历史。在清净寺身上，既留存了泉州海外贸易的发展印记，又刻写着泉州伊斯兰宗教文化的历史缩影，更折射出中阿文化交流的绚烂篇章。

穆斯林在清净寺做礼拜。（陈英杰 摄）
Muslims were praying at Qingjing Mosque. (Photo by Chen Yingjie)

Qingjing Mosque has witnessed the life of Quanzhou's Muslim merchants and their clans in the Song and Yuan Dynasties. They were the major drivers for Asian maritime trade and the diverse social structure of the port city at that time. The style and elements of the mosque show the convergence of people and cultural coexistence in Quanzhou brought by maritime trade, and enriched the composition and cultural significance of the port city. Additionally, Qingjing Mosque was initially located outside the city, but as the foreign merchant settlements grew in the 12th and 13th centuries, the city expanded southward. Naturally, the mosque was incorporated into the downtown. Qingjing Mosque is not only a precious relic of Quanzhou foreign merchant community during the Song and Yuan Dynasties, but also an important landmark of commercial downtown, indicating the unique convergence and evolution of the port city at that time.

Relentless efforts of local communities have helped the protection of Qingjing Mosque. It is their genuine affection and appreciation that ensures the preservation of the mosque's architecture and cultural relics. The spatial layout, weathered bricks and stones preserved in Qingjing Mosque and the engraved patterns and inscriptions on the stones, allow us to explore the distant history. Qingjing Mosque not only bears the imprint of Quanzhou's overseas trade but also gives us a historical glimpse of Quanzhou's Islamic culture, reflecting the brilliant chapter of Sino-Arabic cultural exchange.

在清净寺里参加活动的穆斯林。（陈英杰 摄）
Muslims participating in an activity at Qingjing Mosque. (Photo by Chen Yingjie)

泉州穆斯林的节庆与礼俗

宋元时期来自阿拉伯与波斯地区的穆斯林和泉州本土文化长期接触所产生的交流、碰撞与融合，以及由此引起的生活习俗、宗教信仰、价值观念、艺术形态、婚姻与家族血统的一系列变化，这从泉州穆斯林家族编修族谱、与汉人通婚以及墓葬等形式中均可以得到印证。

历代泉州城内的穆斯林围绕清真寺聚族而居，尤以黄、马、夏等姓氏最为集中。明清以后，穆斯林家族后裔逐渐分散出去，在各乡村形成宗族组织。今天，居住在清净寺周边的穆斯林依然传承着伊斯兰风俗习惯，保留开斋节、古尔邦节、圣纪节等节庆活动。其他迁居乡村的穆斯林后裔，在本土化过程中保留伊斯兰文化的集体记忆和历史记忆，这也吸引着国内外众多穆斯林前来探访。

开斋节，是伊斯兰教三大重要宗教节日之一。在开斋节这天，泉州的穆斯林会准备一种最具特色的食品“油香”，它以色黄、味香、酥软而闻名。相传这一美食是元代由波斯的布哈拉、伊斯法罕等地传入。泉州穆斯林凡遇婚丧节庆，均以油香作为点心招待亲友。

穆斯林在奉天坛做礼拜。（成冬冬 摄）
Muslims were praying in Fengtian Altar. (Photo by Cheng Dongdong)

The Festivals, Etiquette and Customs of Muslims in Quanzhou

During the Song and Yuan Dynasties, there were extensive interactions and integration between Muslims from Arab and Persian regions and the people of Quanzhou, which resulted in a series of transformations in customs, religious beliefs, values, art forms, marriage practices, and family lineage. Evidence of these changes can be seen through the compiled genealogies of Quanzhou's Muslim families, their intermarriage with the Han people and burial customs.

Throughout history, Muslims families with surnames mainly Huang, Ma, Xia, and others in downtown Quanzhou have gathered around mosques, living as a community. After the Ming and Qing Dynasties, the descendants of Muslim families gradually dispersed and formed clans in various villages. Today, Muslims living around Qingjing Mosque inherit Islamic customs and celebrate festivals such as Eid al-Fitr, Eid al-Adha, and Mawlid. The descendants of Muslims who migrated to rural areas have retained collective memories and historical consciousness of Islamic culture in localization. This also attracts many Muslim visitors from both China and abroad.

Eid al-Fitr presents one of the three most important religious festivals in Islam. On that day, Muslims will prepare a lavish feast with *Youxiang* as the most distinctive dessert. Renowned for its golden color, enticing aroma, and crispy texture, it is said that *Youxiang* entered China from Bukhara, Isfahan, and other places in the Yuan Dynasty. Muslims in Quanzhou still have the tradition to treat guests with *Youxiang* at weddings or funerals.

在清净寺参加活动的穆斯林。（张清杰 摄）
Muslims participating an activity in Qingjing Mosque. (Photo by Zhang Qingjie)

泉州本土制作油香的原料有面粉、白糖、芝麻、冬瓜糖、炒花生末、鸡蛋等。油香种类很多，讲究也不少：糯米油香，是吉祥、幸福的象征；面粉甜油香，是安乐、欢庆的象征；面粉咸油香，是表达对已故亲人的怀念，主要用于正忌；薯粉油香，用于娩忌，仅作本家纪念，不可分送亲友客人；地瓜油香，表达对亡人的极度哀痛，用于回民死亡出殡后食用。开斋节当天的食品还有油酥花茧、油酥脆花等。

开斋节当天，穆斯林在“拜斋”后由阿訇带领前往灵山圣墓。他们首先前往三贤四贤墓前行香朝拜，席地而坐，听阿訇诵读《古兰经》，然后各自到先辈或亲属的坟墓前点上安息香悼念亡人，并在旧墓碑文字上描红，再恭请阿訇到坟前念经，为亡魂祈祷。此为泉州穆斯林的扫墓风俗，称为“游坟”。穆斯林从墓地回来后，还会到亲友家祝贺节日愉快。

Youxiang made in Quanzhou is a fried pastry made with flour, sugar, sesame seeds, chopped melon candy, fried and chopped peanuts, and eggs, etc. *Youxiang* comes in many varieties, each with its own symbolic meaning. For example, *Youxiang* made with sticky rice symbolizes good fortune and happiness, a sweet one made of flour signifies peace and celebration, while a salty one made of flour means thinking of the deceased, primarily for commemorating their death anniversary. *Youxiang* made of potato starch is used for commemorating the birthday of the deceased, only for family remembrance, and not served to relatives or guests. Ones crafted from sweet potatoes represent extreme grief for the deceased and are consumed after a Muslim's funeral. On Eid al-Fitr, there are also oil-fried date balls, crispy oil-fried fritters, and other dishes.

On Eid al-Fitr, Akhund leads Muslims to the Islamic Tombs on Lingshan Hill after they break the fast. They first visit the tombs of the two sages to pay their respects and sit down to listen as Akhund recites *Quran*. Then they go to the graves of their ancestors or relatives, lighting benzoin to mourn the deceased. They also add red markings to the old tombstone inscriptions and invite Akhund to pray for the departed souls. The tomb-sweeping custom, or "visiting graves", is a custom of Quanzhou's Muslims. After returning from the cemetery, Muslims also visit their friends and relatives and wish them a happy holiday.

泉州穆斯林在制作油香。（成冬冬 摄）
Quanzhou's Muslims are making *Youxiang*. (Photo by Cheng Dongdong)

穆斯林在开斋节当日前往灵山圣墓游坟。（陈英杰 摄）
On Eid al-Fitr, the Muslims are visiting the Islamic Tombs on Lingshan Hill. (Photo by Chen Yingjie)

来自西亚、中东的穆斯林带来的伊斯兰文化迥异于闽南文化，其充满异国情调的风俗习惯以及独特的婚俗、葬式等，大大丰富了泉州文化的多样性。

南音演奏中所使用的琵琶又被称为“南琶”，是保持唐代形制的曲项琵琶，它最早是在东晋时期由波斯经新疆、甘肃一带传入我国。南琶弹奏时低音淳厚沉抑，中音明快柔和，高音坚实清脆、紧张尖锐。

头巾作为西亚和中东地区的传统服饰，与当地人们的日常生活息息相关。这一佩戴传统也被来泉的阿拉伯人继承下来。在泉州，海边的妇女也一直沿用着红花围巾包扎的阿拉伯式“番巾”。这或许也与伊斯兰侨民留存下来的遗风有关。

传自印度的军持又称“净瓶”，其特征为有流无把，最早属于佛教用器，是云游僧人盛水洗手的用具。军持一词为舶来语，又常被翻译为“捃稚迦”“君墀”“君迟”“军迟”等。《大唐西域记》中有“次南石上则有佛置捃稚迦”。季羡林注：“捃稚迦，梵语‘Knudikā’的音译，意译为水瓶、澡瓶、净瓶、澡罐等也，为僧众十八物之一。”在伊斯兰宗教生活中，用水的场合很多，每日五功之前的“小净”及三餐饭后都需要用水，因此军持也成为伊斯兰教徒常用的器物。南宋时居住在泉州的阿拉伯诗人蒲寿宬写下“明月照我牖，独手携军持”的诗句，反映了军持在日常生活中的作用。

南琶演奏时采用横抱姿势，这有别于现在北琶竖抱的弹奏姿态。（许兆恺 摄）
Southern pipa performers hold the instrument horizontally, in contrast to the vertical position of the northern pipa. (Photo by Xu Zhaokai)

Muslim culture, introduced from West Asia and the Middle East, differs from the customs of Southern Fujian. The exotic practices, unique weddings, and funeral rituals have greatly enriched the cultural heritage of Quanzhou.

The pipa used in Nanyin performances is known as southern pipa. As a curved-neck pipa that keeps the Tang Dynasty form, it came to China from Persia via Xinjiang and Gansu during the Eastern Jin Dynasty (317—420). Southern pipa produces a deep and subdued bass, a lively and soft alto, and a solid, clear, and tense treble.

As a traditional headdress in West Asia and the Middle East, Keffiyeh is incorporated into the daily lives of the local people. This traditional style of wearing a headscarf, known as *fanjin* in Quanzhou, is still used by women living by the seaside. This practice may have been influenced by the cultural heritage of Arab immigrants from West Asia who settled in Quanzhou.

Kundika is a water container with a mouth but without handles for Buddhist monks to wash hands. Kundika is a loanword from India that can be translated into various Chinese characters, such as "捃稚迦" "君墀" "君迟" "军迟". In *The Great Tang Dynasty Record of the Western Regions*, it is mentioned as "捃稚迦 (also known as a bathing bottle, previously known as a military vessel, a mispronunciation)." According to the annotation by Ji Xianlin, a well-known translator and writer in China, "捃稚迦" is a transliteration of the Sanskrit word "Knudikā" and can be translated as a water bottle, bathing bottle, purification bottle, bathing tub, etc. It is one of the eighteen items used by monks. In Islamic religious life, water is used on many occasions, such as the "small purification" before the five daily prayers and after meals. Therefore, Kundika has also become a commonly used item for Muslims. The Arab poet Pu Shoucheng, who lived in Quanzhou during the Southern Song Dynasty, wrote the poem "The bright moon is shining my courtyard; I carry the Kundika with one hand" reflecting the important role of the Kundika in daily life.

宋元时期泉州德化窑与磁灶窑生产的军持在中东和东南亚有广阔的市场。（泉州海外交通史博物馆 供图）

During the Song and Yuan Dynasties, the Kundika produced by Dehua Kiln and Cizao Kiln in Quanzhou had a huge market in the Middle East and Southeast Asia. (Courtesy of Quanzhou Maritime Museum)

根据《诸蕃志》《岛夷志略》等书记录泉州与海外各国往来的商贸情况，宋元以来经由阿拉伯、波斯商人舶运而来福建的有乳香、丁香、安息香、降真香、没药、血竭、阿魏、胡椒、槟榔、龙涎香、腽肭脐等动植物香料药物。正是有这么多香药的传入，使泉州地方日常生活中的用香十分普遍。无怪乎元代诗僧宗泐不禁吟诵出“泉南佛国天下少，满城香气楠檀绕”的诗句来。

永春县达埔镇汉口村的蒲氏家族，其开基祖十三世的蒲世茂，于明代后期从泉州迁至该地，至今已传下十几代子孙。他们以制作香料为业，其制香过程遵循古法工序：香芯沾水、搓香粉、浸水、展香、抡香、切香、晒香、染香脚、晾香，归纳起来的口诀就是：沾、搓、浸、展、抡、切、晒、染、晾九式。这一制香工艺即是由来自阿拉伯的蒲氏家族后裔引进并发展起来的。20 世纪 40 年代，永春蒲氏家族到永春县五里街开设“蒲庆兰香室”，专门成批制作篾香，销往我国港澳地区及马来西亚、印尼、越南等国。如今，永春五里街“蒲庆兰香室”仍保存香壶、碾槽等数代祖传的制作香料器具。

得益于蒲氏家族引进制香工艺，永春的制香业至今仍十分发达。（林建祥 摄）
Thanks to the Pu's family introducing the craft of incense making, the incense-making industry is still highly developed in Yongchun. (Photo by Lin Jianxiang)

Records of Foreign Countries and *A Brief Account of Island Inhabitants* contained the trade between Quanzhou and overseas countries. Since the Song and Yuan Dynasties, Arab and Persian merchants have brought in various aromatic spices and medicinal plants such as frankincense, cloves, benzoin, myrrh, agarwood, bloodroot, valerian, pepper, betel nut, musk, and asafetida. With the introduction of the fragrant medicine, incense was widely accepted by the local people of Quanzhou. No wonder the poet-monk Zongle in the Yuan Dynasty was moved to write the verse "Quanzhou boasts of Pure Lands unrivaled far and wide; the city breathes the scent of eaglewood and sandalwood with joy and pride".

The Pu's family in Hankou Village, Dapu Town, Yongchun County has been making incenses for generations. Pu Shimao, the 13th Pu, moved from Quanzhou downtown to the village in the late Ming Dynasty and started the family's incense trade. Their incense-making process follows ancient techniques: wetting the bamboo core, grinding powder, soaking, spreading, swinging, cutting, sun-drying, dyeing base ends, and drying. The nine steps for short are: wetting, grinding, soaking, spreading, swinging, cutting, drying in the sun, dyeing, and drying. Pu's descendants introduced and developed this craft. In the 1940s, the Pu's family in Yongchun opened Pu Qinglan Incense Shop on Wuli Street, specializing in bamboo incense production which is sold to Chinese Hong Kong, Macao, and to other countries as Malaysia, Indonesia, Vietnam, and beyond. The shop still preserves ancestral utensils like incense pots and grinding troughs used for generations.

永春“蒲庆兰香室”及蒲氏制香。（刘宝生 摄）
Pu Qinglan Incense Shop in Yongchun County and its incense products. (Photo by Liu Baosheng)

阿拉伯书法是阿拉伯文字书写的艺术，其书法讲究节奏感、装饰性和纹样。阿拉伯书法传入中国后，将汉字书法融入阿拉伯书法艺术创作中，并最终形成了具有中国风格的阿拉伯文书法艺术。这其中包括经字画，同时也有中堂、条幅、手卷、对联等中国传统裱褙装帧形式。在泉州穆斯林的居所大门上经常可以看到贴着阿拉伯文对联，而他们的厅堂也常布置阿拉伯文书法挂毯，这些也成为中阿文化交汇融合的象征。

清源山纯阳洞有一段凿刻于元至元四年（1338）的摩崖题刻《重建清源纯阳洞记》，记云："宋季兹山悉毁……我朝至元十有八载，四松僧法昙抚迹吁悼而谋兴复。适心泉蒲公同其弟海云平章协力捐财以资之，规则比于曩时，无虑千百……"石刻中提到的心泉蒲公，指的正是蒲寿庚的哥哥蒲寿宬。他不仅担任过梅州知州，而且雅好诗文，有《心泉学诗稿》存世。这一方面体现出其诗赋成就，同时也可以看出来到泉州的阿拉伯人积极学习、吸收汉文化，以此作为与汉人士大夫交往的一种方式。从这方碑记中我们也可知，在元代，作为穆斯林代表的蒲氏兄弟，也与佛教僧侣、地方官员等积极参与地方文化事业建设，这也从一个侧面体现了泉州多元文化的交融与和谐共处。

泉州穆斯林居所大门的阿拉伯文对联和厅堂中的阿拉伯文书法挂毯。（成冬冬 摄）
The Arabic couplets hanging on gates and Arabic calligraphy hanging in living rooms. (Photo by Cheng Dongdong

Arabic calligraphy, as an Arabic art form, emphasizes rhythm, decoration, and patterns. After its introduction to China, it incorporated Chinese calligraphy into its artistic creation and eventually developed to be with a Chinese style. For example, it borrowed traditional Chinese mounting and framing like central scrolls, horizontal scrolls, hand scrolls, and couplets, as well as incorporating the aesthetic of Chinese brush painting into its scripture writing. In local Muslim households, Arabic couplets are commonly seen on gates while Arabic calligraphy hangs in living rooms. It symbolizes the blending of Chinese and Arabic cultures.

A cliff inscription called *Record of Rebuilding Chunyang Cave in Qingyuan Mountain* was carved in 1338 of the Yuan Dynasty. It notes "During the Song Dynasty, this cave was totally destroyed... Since the beginning of the Yuan Dynasty, Monk Fatan from Sisong Temple lamented the ruins and planned renovation. Xinquan Pugong and his brother donated funds. The layout remains the same as before." Xinquan Pugong mentioned in the inscription refers to Pu Shoucheng, the elder brother of Pu Shougeng. Serving as the Prefect of Meizhou, he has a passion for poetry and literature. His collection of poems, *Xinquan Poetry*, still exists. This not only reflects his own achievements in poetry but also shows that the Quanzhou Arabs were actively studying and absorbing Chinese culture to interact with Chinese literati and officials. From this inscription, it can be seen that during the Yuan Dynasty, the Pu brothers, representatives of Muslims, actively participated in the construction of local cultural projects, along with Buddhist monks and local officials. This reflects the blending and harmonious coexistence of diverse cultures in Quanzhou.

《重建清源纯阳洞记》题刻中提到的心泉蒲公，正是蒲寿庚的哥哥蒲寿宬。（成冬冬 摄）

Xinquan Pugong mentioned in *Record of Rebuilding Chunyang Cave in Qingyuan Mountain* refers to Pu Shoucheng, Pu Shougeng's elder brother. (Photo by Cheng Dongdong)

有着近 600 年历史的陈埭丁氏宗祠将伊斯兰装饰与传统闽南建筑风格相融合。（成冬冬、施清凉 摄）
The Ding's Ancestral Hall in Chendai Town, with a nearly 600-year history, integrates Islamic decorative elements and traditional Southern Fujian architectural style. (Photo by Cheng Dongdong & Shi Qingliang)

百代瞻依
丁氏大宗祠

清净光明，摩尼光佛——草庵摩尼光佛造像

The Statue of Mani in Cao’an Temple: a Symbol of Purity and Light

从波斯到泉州

From Persia to Quanzhou

结草为庵：深藏山中的石造像

Cao’ an Temple Consecrating the Stone Statue on the Hill

古井中发现的“明教会”碗

The “Mingjiao Hui” Bowl Discovered in the Ancient Well

位于晋江华表山东麓的草庵，是 20 世纪 50 年代被泉州历史学者吴文良先生重新发现的宋元时期华化摩尼教（又称明教）寺庙遗址，其至晚创建于 10—11 世纪的北宋初期，初为草构，故名为“草庵”。草庵摩尼光佛造像作为宋元泉州摩尼教传播的重要见证，是世界上唯一保存下来的摩尼教教主石刻造像。摩尼光佛造像“道貌佛身”的形象是这一外来宗教寓于本土信仰进行融合式传播的结果，也是异域文化和本土文化的独特对话，展现了宋元时期泉州作为世界海洋商贸中心强大的文化包容力。

Cao'an Temple, located at the eastern foot of Huabiao Hill in Jinjiang, was rediscovered by Wu Wenliang, a Quanzhou historian, in the 1950s as the site of a Manichaeism (also known as "Mingjiao" or the Religion of Light) temple in the Song-Yuan era. Cao'an Temple was built not later than the 10th and 11th centuries in the early Northern Song Dynasty. It was so named as it was originally a straw hut ("Cao'an" means "straw hut" in Chinese). As an important witness to the spread of Manichaeism in Quanzhou during the Song and Yuan Dynasties, the statue is the world's only extant stone statue of Mani. The statue of Mani with its "Taoist appearance but Buddhist body", is the outcome of the fusion of this foreign religion with local beliefs and of the unique dialogue between the foreign and local cultures, showing the strong cultural inclusiveness of Quanzhou as the world's emporium in the Song-Yuan era.

草庵位于泉州城以南 15 千米的华表山东麓，依山而筑，是宋元时期泉州城远郊的一处摩尼教寺院。（陈英杰 摄）

Cao'an Temple, a Manichaean temple in the outer suburbs of Quanzhou City in the Song-Yuan era, lies at the eastern foot of Huabiao Hill, 15 kilometers away from the south of Quanzhou City. (Photo by Chen Yingjie)

从波斯到泉州

源于古代波斯地区的摩尼教是中古时期的世界性宗教，也是古代中国的一大外来宗教。公元 3 世纪中叶，摩尼教由波斯人摩尼所创立，此后迅速传播至亚洲、欧洲和北非等地区。公元 6—7 世纪，摩尼教从陆上丝绸之路传入新疆，随后又由新疆传至中原。据《佛祖统纪》记载，公元 694 年“波斯国人拂多诞持《二宗经》伪教来朝”。

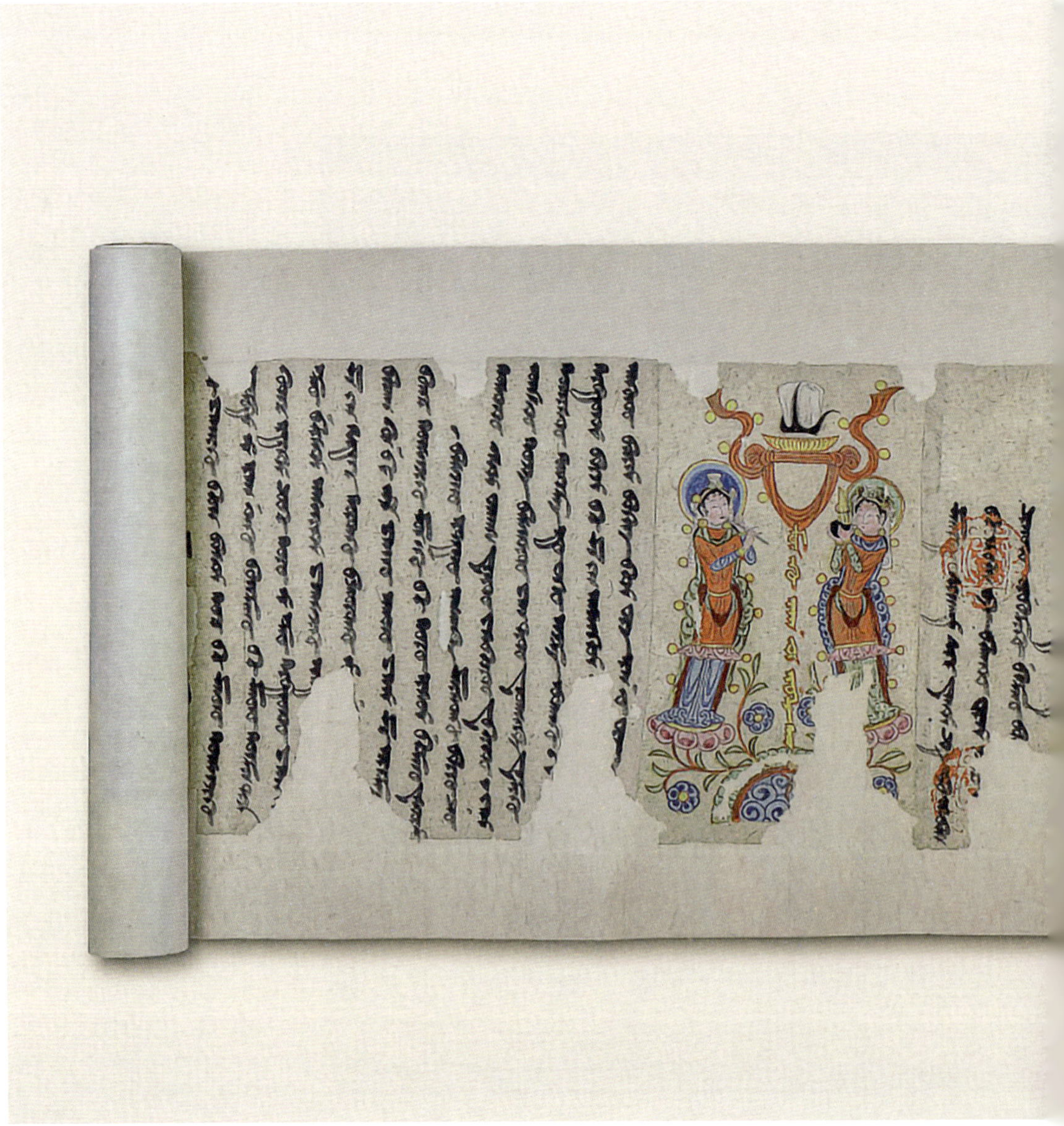

From Persia to Quanzhou

Manichaeism originated in ancient Persia. It was a world religion in the Middle Ages and a main foreign religion in ancient China. It was founded by Mani, a Persian, in the middle of the 3rd century and then spread rapidly to Asia, Europe and North Africa. In the 6th and 7th centuries, Manichaeism was introduced to Xinjiang Province via the Silk Road, and subsequently to the Central Plains. According to *The Chronicle of the Buddhas and the Patriarchs*, "In 694, a Persian man named Furstadan brought the book of *The Shabuhragan* and a quasi-religion to the nation."

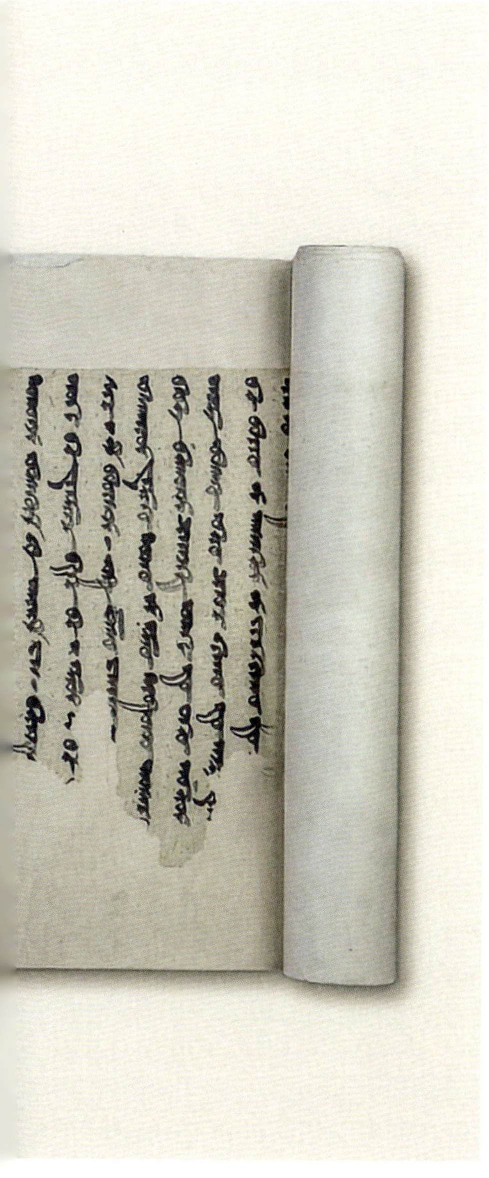

1981年新疆吐鲁番柏孜克里克出土的粟特文摩尼教徒书信。（闽人 供图）

In 1981, the letters of the Manichaeans in Sogdian script were unearthed in Bezeklik, Turpan, Xinjiang. (Courtesy of Minren)

元代管理江南诸路明教、秦教的失里门主教墓碑。（成冬冬 摄）
The tombstone of the Shilimen Bishop who administered the Manichaeism and Nestorianism in regions south of the Yangtze River during the Yuan Dynasty. (Photo by Cheng Dongdong)

唐大历三年（768）至元和二年（807），摩尼教教众先后在长安（今陕西西安）、荆州、扬州、洪州（今江西南昌）、越州（今浙江绍兴）、河南府(今河南洛阳)、太原府等地建立寺院，并获赐额“大云光明寺”。唐会昌年间，武宗灭佛，摩尼教被禁止在华传播，有摩尼教法师南逃入闽，由此摩尼教传至泉州。关于摩尼教的入泉因由与路线，何乔远在《闽书》中也有过记载：“会昌中，汰僧，明教在汰中。有呼禄法师者，来入福唐（今福州福清），授侣三山（今福州），游方泉郡，卒葬郡北山（今泉州清源山）下。”近年所发现的闽东霞浦文书，进一步证实了这一传播路径。及至元代，朝廷在泉州专门设有管理明教和秦教（即景教）的主教官。据文献记载，东南沿海的宋元摩尼教寺还有慈溪的崇寿宫、苍南选真寺和平阳潜光院等，但只有晋江草庵保存下来，更显弥足珍贵。

摩尼教的教义，主要是以波斯的琐罗亚斯德教为基础，同时融合了基督教、诺斯替教、佛教的教义，逐渐形成以“二宗三际”为核心的信仰体系。所谓“二宗”指的是光明与黑暗，也即善与恶，其教义认为未有天地之时，只有善恶二宗。“三际”则指初际、中际和后际，也即指过去、现在和未来。摩尼认为未有天地之前，也即世界处于初际阶段，明暗是分开的；此后，黑暗开始侵入光明并进行斗争，随之两者混合，而天地和人类是两者混合的产物，世界遂进入中际阶段，摩尼教创立的目的是使世人的灵魂得到超脱，同时也为早日摆脱黑暗的纠缠重新回归光明；摩尼认为世界末日终将到来，届时明暗又将重新分开，此即后际阶段。由此可见摩尼教的教义是以光明与黑暗斗争的二元论作为主旨思想。

From 768 to 807 of the Tang Dynasty, Manichaeans established temples in Chang'an (Xi'an in Shaanxi Province nowadays), Jingzhou, Yangzhou, Hongzhou (Nanchang in Jiangxi Province nowadays), Yuezhou (Shaoxing in Zhejiang Province nowadays), Henan Prefecture (Luoyang in Henan Province nowadays), and Taiyuan Prefecture. They were imperially granted as "Dayun Guangming Temple". However, during 841 and 846, Emperor Wuzong (814—846), an ardent follower of Taoism, issued a series of decrees to suppress Buddhism and other religions, including Manichaeism. Therefore, some Manichaean priests fled southward to Fujian, and spread their faith to Quanzhou. With regards to the reason and route of Manichaeism to Quanzhou, He Qiaoyuan mentioned in *The Book of Min*, "During 841 to 846, Buddhism and other religions were suppressed, and Manichaeism was no exception. Therefore, Hulu Master, who fled to Fuqing in Fujian Province, introduced Manichaeism to Fuzhou. He preached Manichaeism around Quanzhou, and finally was buried at the foot of Qingyuan Mountain in Quanzhou." In recent years, Xiapu Documents found in eastern Fujian, have confirmed this account. In the Yuan Dynasty, the imperial court appointed officials in Quanzhou to manage Manichaeism and Nestorianism. According to the documents, there were other Manichaean temples on the southeast coast during the Song-Yuan era, such as Chongshou Palace in Cixi, Xuanzhen Temple in Cangnan, and Qianguang Institute in Pingyang, but only Cao'an Temple in Jinjiang has survived until today, making it a rare and valuable relic.

While integrating the doctrines of Christianity, Gnosticism and Buddhism, the Manichaeism doctrines, mainly based on the Persian Zoroastrianism, gradually developed the belief system with the "theory of two substances and three-time periods" as its core. The "two substances" refer to light and darkness, symbolizing good and evil. The "three periods" refer to the initial, middle, and last stages or the past, present, and future. Mani holds that before the creation of heaven and earth, there were only good and evil. The world was in the initial stage, when light and darkness were separate. After that, darkness began to invade and struggle with light, and then the two mixed, creating heaven, earth, and human beings. Later, the world entered the middle stage. Manichaeism was set up to bring human beings' spirits detached from this world, and to escape from darkness and return to light as soon as possible. Mani believed that the world would end and that the light and darkness would be separated again, which was the last stage. This clarifies that Manichaeanism was based on the dualism of the struggle between light and darkness.

摩尼教宇宙图。（闽人 供图）
Manichaeism's Diagram of the Universe. (Courtesy of Minren)

结草为庵：深藏山中的石造像

位于晋江华表山东麓的草庵，是宋元时期泉州城远郊的一处摩尼教寺。雕凿于草庵寺石室正中崖壁上的摩尼光佛造像，是目前世界上仅存的摩尼教创始人的石雕造像。明代何乔远在《闽书》中提到："华表山，与灵源山相连，两峰角立如华表。山背之麓，有草庵，元时物也，祀摩尼佛。"清乾隆《晋江县志》亦载："华表山在五都，距城南四十里，双峰角立如华表，然麓有草庵，元时建祀摩尼佛。"

元至元五年（1339），依山崖傍筑的草庵由信众捐资改主体建筑为石构，现存栌斗、石柱、梁架等形制为元代风格。明万历年间，黄凤翔于秋日访草庵，留下诗句："琳宫秋日共跻登，木落山空爽气澄。细草久湮仙峤路，斜晖暂作佛坛灯。竹边泉脉邻丹灶，洞里云根蔓绿藤。飘瓦颓垣君莫问，萧然一榻便崚嶒。"

20 世纪 30 年代利用元代原石构件，又扩建了外檐部分，在保持原有规制的基础上，进深扩一间。现今我们看到的建筑形式为面阔三间，进深两间，单檐歇山顶，饰以燕尾脊，外墙则以红砖饰面。

草庵主体建筑。（刘宝生 摄）
The main building of Cao'an Temple. (Photo by Liu Baosheng)

Cao'an Temple Consecrating the Stone Statue on the Hill

Located at the eastern foot of Huabiao Hill in Jinjiang, Cao'an Temple was a Manichaean temple on the far outskirts of Quanzhou during the Song and Yuan Dynasties. The Statue of Mani, carved into the cliff wall in the middle of the stone room of the temple, is the only extant stone statue of the founder of Manichaeism in the world. He Qiaoyuan wrote in *The Book of Min*, "Huabiao Hill connects Lingyuan Hill, and their two peaks stand at an angle like an ornamental column. At the foot of the back of the hill, there is a grass nunnery, built in the Yuan Dynasty, dedicated to Mani." In *Chronicle of Jinjiang County* compiled during Emperor Qianlong's reign also showed: "Huabiao Hill is in Wudu, about 20 kilometers away from the south of Quanzhou City, with two peaks standing at an angle like an ornamental column. There is Cao'an Temple at the foot of the hill, which was built in the Yuan Dynasty to worship Mani."

In 1339 of the Yuan Dynasty, the worshipers donated money to rebuild the main building of Cao'an Temple on the cliff as a stone structure. The existing cap block, stone pillars and beams were in the style of the Yuan Dynasty. During 1573 and 1620 of the Ming Dynasty, Huang Fengxiang visited Cao'an Temple in autumn and composed a poem: "In autumn, I climbed up this beautiful place. Trees were under my feet and the air was refreshing. Submerged the fine grass was in the road to the fairy mountain for a long time, and a Buddhist altar lamp the slanting light seemed like. The temple was adjacent to bamboos, spring, and the alchemy furnace. Green vines entwined along the temple. You'd better ignore its ruined tiles and walls; desolation reigns in a single bed, lofty and precipitous."

In the 1930s, based on the original stone construction in the Yuan Dynasty, the outer eaves were expanded to one *chien* long. Consequently, the current building is three-*chien* wide and two-*chien* long, with a single eave and a saddle roof, dovetail ridge decoration, and a red brick facade.

庵前平台为石柱和石板架空的高台。紧挨石室东侧增建有面阔一间的两层平屋面阁楼石构僧舍，与石室左门相通。石室右前方有一座面阔三间、进深一间的三川脊石构凉亭。阁楼和凉亭采用绿釉或彩绘白釉瓶式栏杆，具有中西合璧的风格和民国时期特征。凉亭、庙宇、僧舍一字排开，高低错落，构成草庵的主体建筑群。

草庵改为石构的同一年，信众也在庵内的崖壁上雕刻出摩尼光佛造像。圆龛直径 1.68 米，意在象征日形和月形。这与摩尼教“朝拜日，夕拜月”的义理吻合，也正因崇拜日月，民间遂将之称为“明教”。

摩尼光佛造像高 1.54 米，宽 0.83 米，其面相丰满，神态安详，耳大垂肩，颔下有两撮长须下垂，身着宽袖对衽长袍，胸襟打结带，结带用圆饰套束蝴蝶形，衣褶简朴流畅，结跏趺坐于莲花座上，背雕十八道毫光四射纹饰，这与摩尼教崇尚光明的教义相契合。

草庵内外景。（刘宝生 摄）
The interior and exterior views of Cao'an Temple. (Photo by Liu Baosheng)

In front of Cao'an Temple is a raised platform with stone pillars and slabs. Adjacent to the east side of the stone room, a two-story flat roof attic was built, which was a stone-made monk's house and connected to the left door of the stone room. To the right of the stone room, there is a stone pavilion with three-*chien* wide and one-*chien* deep with a three-section ridge. The attic and the pavilion are decorated with green glaze or painted white glaze vase-style balustrades in Chinese and Western styles and with characteristics of the Republican era. The pavilion, the temple and the monks' house are lined up in a row, highly and lowly scattered, forming the main building complex of Cao'an Temple.

In the same year when Cao'an Temple was converted into a stone building, the worshipers also carved a statue of Mani on the cliff of Cao'an Temple. The round niche, 1.68 meters in diameter, represents the sun and the moon, following the Manichaean principle of "worshiping the sun in the morning and the moon in the evening". Because they worship the sun and the moon, it is also known as the "Ming Religion" [In Chinese, the character of " 明 " (bright) is composed of " 日 " (sun) and " 月 " (moon)].

Sitting cross-legged on a lotus seat, the Statue of Mani is 1.54 meters high and 0.83 meters wide, with a plump, serene face, big ears, and shoulders, two long beards hanging down from his jaw, wearing a long robe with wide sleeves and a knotted belt on the bosom, the knotted belt in the butterfly pattern with a rounded ornament. His wearing is simple and plain and his back is carved with the motif of 18 radiant beams, in keeping with Manichaean teachings of the worship of light.

草庵摩尼光佛石刻造像与泉州本土的佛、道信仰融合，创造了“道貌佛身”的摩尼形象。这一佛化、道化过程，体现了入华摩尼教“三圣同一”的思想。（成冬冬 摄）

The stone statue of Mani in Cao'an Temple was influenced by Quanzhou's indigenous Buddhism and Taoism, presenting a Mani figure with a Taoist appearance but Buddhist body. The Buddhist and Taoist transformation demonstrates the idea of the "unity of the three saints" in the adaptation of Manichaeism to China. (Photo by Cheng Dongdong)

此外，草庵摩尼光佛形象与敦煌出土的唐代写本摩尼教重要经典《摩尼光佛教法仪略》中所描述的“摩尼光佛顶圆十二光王胜相，体备大明，无量秘义；妙形特绝，人天无比；串以素帔，仿四净法身；其居白座，像五金刚地；二界合离，初后旨趣，宛在真容，观之可晓。诸有灵相，百千胜妙，实难备陈。”基本形似，亦有契合之妙。

草庵还保存了较为完整的摩尼教教义和仪轨的系列物证，比如记事石刻、劝念石刻等。在摩尼光佛圆龛左上角阴刻：“谢店市信士陈真泽立寺，喜舍本师圣像，祈荐考妣早生佛地者。至元五年戌月四日记。”右上角则阴刻：“兴化路罗山境姚兴祖，奉舍石室一完。祈荐先君正卿姚汝坚三十三宴，妣郭氏五九太孺，继母黄十三娘，先兄姚月涧，四学世生界者。”这些文字具有丰富的历史信息，是目前草庵立寺时间、立寺人、摩尼光佛石雕像镌刻时间和石构建筑始建年代最可靠的原始文字记载。

草庵旁的石壁上还刻有摩尼教“四寂法身”信条：“劝念清净、光明、大力、智慧，无上至真，摩尼光佛，正统乙丑九月十三日，住山弟子明书立。”现石刻为后来根据照片重新复刻。在泉州海外交通史博物馆中也收藏了一方“大力”石刻。

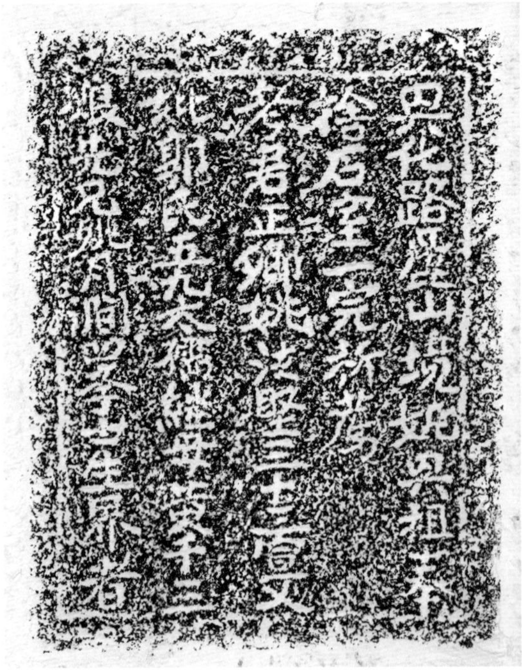

草庵纪年记事题刻拓片。（成冬冬 摄）
The rubbings of the chronicle and recording inscription in Cao’an Temple. (Photo by Cheng Dongdong)

In addition, the Statue of Mani in Cao'an Temple basically matches the description of Mani's image in the important classic of Manichaeism in the Tang Dynasty unearthed at Dunhuang, which was *A Summary of Manichaeism Laws*. It describes, "The statue of Mani has a round top of twelve light beams, meaning great wisdom and boundless secrets. Its shape is extraordinary and incomparable. Wearing a plain cape, it looks like the four-pure Dharmakya. Its white seat is like that of five Buddha's warrior attendants. Darkness and light mingled or separated, after the beginning of purport, like its real appearance, so it can be known through viewing. There are all kinds of spiritual signs, thousands of subtleties, which are difficult to be described." The statue's shape generally corresponds to the descriptions and is a marvelous fit.

Cao'an Temple also preserves a relatively complete series of physical evidence of Manichaean doctrines and rituals, such as stone inscriptions for notation and exhortation. In the upper left-hand corner of the round niche of the statue of Mani was incised "Chen Zhenze, a worshiper in Xiedian, donated money to establish the temple and the holy image of the Master to pray to Buddha for the early arrival of his parents' detachment. In lunar September 4, 1339 of the Yuan Dynasty." In the upper right-hand corner, the inscription reads: "Yao Xingzu from Luoshan, Xinghua, dedicated to the completion of a stone room to pray for the deceased Yao Rujian, 33 years old, his mother Guo surname 59 years old, his stepmother Huang Shisanniang, his late brother Yao Yuejian, these four departed." These texts contain rich historical information and are the most reliable original written records suggesting Cao'an Temple's establishing time, its establishers and the engraving time of the statue and the stone structure's initial building time.

On the stone wall next to Cao'an Temple was also engraved the Manichaean creed of "Four Dharma Bodies": "Exhorting to pursuing purity, light, great strength and wisdom. Supreme to the truth the Statue of Mani. Erected by Ming Shu (the host in the temple) on the 13th day of lunar September in 1445 of the Yuan Dynasty." The inscription was later re-carved after a photo. Quanzhou Maritime Museum also has a stone inscription with "Dali (great strength)".

草庵“劝念”摩崖石刻和泉州海外交通史博物馆馆藏的“大力”石刻。（成冬冬 摄）
The cliff inscription of the "exhortation" at Cao'an Temple and the stone inscription with "Dali" (great strength) collected in Quanzhou Maritime Museum. (Photo by Cheng Dongdong)

20 世纪 30 年代，弘一法师曾先后三次住锡草庵，每次淹留累月，或度岁，或养病，或弘法。其间，弘一法师为重兴的草庵石室大门、金柱等撰书 4 副对联，其冠字联为：“草藏不除，便觉眼前生意满；庵门常掩，毋忘世上苦人多。”此外，他还写下一篇《重兴草庵记》，记述草庵的历史沿革与重兴过程。文中提到：“草庵肇兴，盖在宋代，逮及明初，轮奂尽美……殿供石佛，昔为岩壁，常现金容，因依其形，创造石像。余题句云，‘石壁光明，相传为文佛现影；史乘记载，于此有名贤读书。’”

在距离草庵一千米许的苏内村，还有一所供奉摩尼教神祇的境主宫（即水尾宫），为 20 世纪 30 年代重建。境主宫寝殿墙壁上绘制有“五境主”，居中者为摩尼光佛，左为都天灵相（又称灵圣公），右为秦皎明使（亦称千春公），外侧则分别为境主公和十八真人。由此可见摩尼教逐渐融入当地人生活的华化过程中。

In the 1930s, Master Hongyi lived in Cao'an Temple three times, each time for several months. He either celebrated the Chinese New Year there, or recuperated, or preached. During his stay, he wrote four couplets for the main door of the stone room and the golden pillars of the renovated Cao'an Temple, one of which reads, "The grass grows wild and shows vitality. Although the door is always closed, one should not forget that many sufferers are in the outside world." He also wrote *The Record of the Renovation of Cao'an Temple*, which traced the history of Cao'an Temple and its renovation process. In this article, it is mentioned that "Cao'an Temple was founded in the Song Dynasty, and by the beginning of the Ming Dynasty, it had become a beautiful place ... Cao'an Temple dedicated to the stone Buddha used to be a rock wall and often had a golden appearance, so the stone statue was sculpted according to its shape. I inscribed the sentence: 'The stone wall was bright. It was said to be the manifestation of Buddha's shadow. According to history, famous sages once studied here.'"

In Sunei Village, about a kilometer away from Cao'an Temple, there is another shrine dedicated to the Manichaean deities, which is called Jingzhu Palace (or Shuiwei Palace) and was rebuilt in the 1930s. On the walls of the chambers were painted five Jingzhu. In the center stands the Statue of Mani, to his left and right are Dutianlingxiang (also known as Lingshenggong) and Qinjiaomingshi (also known as Qianchungong) and the Lord of the Realm and the Eighteen Immortals on the outside. This shows the process of Manichaeism's gradually integrating into local people's life.

弘一法师为草庵题写的冠字对联。（林清哲 摄）

The couplet written by Master Hongyi with Chinese characters " 草 " (meaning "grass") and "庵" (meaning "nunnery or monastery") as the first character. (Photo by Lin Qingzhe)

过去的数十年里，草庵及摩尼光佛造像引起了世界的关注。1986 年，瑞典隆德大学的摩尼教学者翁拙瑞博士到草庵进行实地考察。1987 年 8 月，首届国际摩尼教学术讨论会在瑞典隆德大学举行，并以翁拙瑞博士拍摄的草庵摩尼光佛石造像作为会徽。翁拙瑞博士在大会上还向与会学者放映了他制作的草庵考察幻灯片。泉州这一摩尼教遗址正式展现在国际摩尼教学界面前。

1991 年，联合国教科文组织海上丝绸之路考察团在参观草庵后，成员们抑制不住内心欣喜，盛赞草庵摩尼光佛造像是“世界唯一的”，并将之列为“海上丝绸之路考察活动的最大发现、最大成就”。2004 年，金庸先生到访草庵，谈及《倚天屠龙记》的撰写过程时称“明教不是我杜撰的”。

In the past few decades, Cao'an Temple and the Statue of Mani have attracted people's attention all over the world. In 1986, Dr. Peter Bryder, a Manichaean scholar from Lund University, Sweden, made a field trip to Cao'an Temple. In August 1987, the First International Manichaeism Symposium was held at Lund University, Sweden, and adopted the Statue of Mani as the emblem. Peter Bryder also showed his Cao'an Temple expedition to the scholars at the conference with a slide projector, formally introducing this Manichaean site in Quanzhou to the international Manichaean community.

After visiting Cao'an Temple in 1991, the members of the UNESCO's Maritime Silk Road mission could not contain their delight and praised the Statue of Mani as "the unique (statue) in the world" and listed it as "the greatest discovery and achievement of their Maritime Silk Road expedition". In 2004, Louis Cha visited Cao'an Temple and shared the process of writing the novel *Heaven Sword and Dragon Sabre*, saying that "I did not make up the Manichaeism".

1991 年，联合国教科文组织“海上丝绸之路”考察团参观草庵，给予其极高评价。（成冬冬 摄）
In 1991, the UNESCO's Maritime Silk Road mission visited Cao'an Temple and praised it highly. (Photo by Cheng Dongdong)

古井中发现的“明教会”碗

1979 年，于草庵前 20 米处重建龙泉书院时，工人在挖地基之际发现一口古井，井中发掘出土一件“明教会”褐釉碗和几十块残片。该碗为磁灶窑产品，口径 18.5 厘米、高 6.5 厘米、底高 0.08 厘米，敞口浅腹，低圈足露胎，内施酱褐色釉，外施半釉，碗内壁阴刻行书“明教会”三字。在几十块残片中，还有 13 片阴刻了“明”“教”“会”字样，这种统一制式的瓷碗表明当时有不少摩尼教教徒活跃于此。作为当地教众统一烧制的食具，“明教会”碗是当时泉州摩尼教兴盛的一个重要标志。

经考古学者进行窑址调查，最终确定烧制“明教会”碗的就是磁灶窑系的大树威窑。该窑址同样出土了刻有“明”“教”“会”字样的残片，说明草庵“明教会”碗是以订烧方式生产，且经鉴定年代为北宋。“明教会”碗为北宋摩尼教在草庵有组织的结社活动提供了实物见证，被定为国家一级文物。

从草庵所保存下来的摩尼光佛造像、教义和仪轨的石刻、建筑以及器物等系列物证，呈现出摩尼教在中国的本土化特征，是摩尼教在中国传播与发展的珍贵见证，体现出 10—14 世纪古刺桐港多元文化交流融合的重要社会特质。

出土宋“明教会”碗的古井及出土碑。（成冬冬 摄）

The ancient well where the “明教会” bowl was excavated and the excavated stele. (Photo by Cheng Dongdong)

The "Mingjiao Hui" Bowl Discovered in the Ancient Well

In 1979, when Longquan Academy was rebuilt in the spot 20 meters in front of Cao'an Temple, an ancient well was discovered when the workers were digging the foundations. A brown glazed bowl engraved with the Chinese characters " 明教会 " ("Mingjiao Hui", literally meaning " Society of the Religion of Light") and dozens of fragments were unearthed from the well. The bowl had an open mouth and shallow belly, a low base rim, glazed inside in a soy-brown color and half-glazed outside. The inside of the bowl was engraved with Chinese characters " 明教会 ". This bowl was 18.5cm in diameter, 6.5cm in height, and 0.08cm in height at the base, which was a product of Cizao Kilns. Among the dozens of fragments, thirteen were engraved with the Chinese characters " 明 ", " 教 " or " 会 ", suggesting that the "明教会" bowls were produced in custom-burning method in the Northern Song Dynasty. This style of porcelain bowl provided evidence of the activity of Manichaeism in Cao'an Temple. The bowl, produced in a bespoke manner by local believers for eating, was a significant symbol of the prosperity of the Manichaeism in Quanzhou.

Archaeologists examined the kiln site and identified that it was Dashuwei Kiln belonging to Cizao Kilns that produced the " 明教会 " bowl. The kiln site also produced fragments inscribed with the characters" 明 ", " 教 " and " 会 ", suggesting that the " 明教会 " bowl was produced in a bespoke manner during the Northern Song Dynasty. The "明教会" bowl designated as a national cultural relic provides physical evidence of the organized association of Manichaeism in Cao'an Temple in the Northern Song Dynasty.

The Statue of Mani, stone inscriptions of doctrines and rituals, architecture and artifacts preserved in Cao'an Temple demonstrate the localization of Manichaeism in China. They are precious testimony to the transmission and development of Manichaeism in China, reflecting important social characteristics of the multicultural exchange and fusion of the ancient Zayton Port from the 10th to 14th centuries.

现藏于晋江博物馆的宋代"明教会"碗。（成冬冬 摄）

The " 明教会 " bowl from the Song Dynasty is stored in Jinjiang Museum now. (Photo by Cheng Dongdong)

结　语

“泉州：宋元中国的世界海洋商贸中心”，她既以风樯鳞集的国际性港埠承载着海洋商贸的奇迹，也以多元共生的文化景观创造了不同文明交流互鉴的典范。她书写了古代中国与世界交互影响的历史记忆，也为构建人类命运共同体前行之路，带来那来自岁月深处的思索、智慧与启示……

Conclusion

Quanzhou: Emporium of the World in Song-Yuan China, not only has worked miracles for maritime trade with its bustling international port, but also is a model of cultural diversity and exchanges with its rich and mutual cultural heritages. It has the historical memory for the interaction between ancient China and the outside world, and brings us with the contemplation, wisdom and inspiration for building a human community with a shared future.

泉州湾出海口。（许兆恺 摄）
The estuary of Quanzhou Bay. (Photo by Xu Zhaokai)

参考文献

[1] 脱脱 . 宋史 [M]. 北京：中华书局，1977.

[2] 徐松 . 宋会要辑稿 [M]. 北京：中华书局，1957.

[3] 李心传，胡坤 . 建炎以来系年要录 [M]. 北京：中华书局，2013.

[4] 黄仲昭 . 八闽通志 [M]. 福州：福建人民出版社，2017.

[5] 何乔远 . 闽书 [M]. 福州：福建人民出版社，1995.

[6] 阳思谦，徐敏学，吴维新 .（万历）泉州府志 [M]. 台北：学生书局，1987.

[7] 怀荫布，黄任，郭赓武 .（乾隆）泉州府志 [M]. 上海：上海书店出版社，2000.

[8] 胡之鋘，周学曾、尤逊恭 .（道光）晋江县志 [M]. 上海：上海书店出版社，2000.

[9] [英] 崔瑞德，[美] 史乐民 . 剑桥中国宋代史 [M]. 北京：中国社会科学出版社，2018.

[10] 苏基朗 . 刺桐梦华录：近世前期闽南的市场经济 946-1368 [M]. 杭州：浙江大学出版社，2012.

[11] 吴文良，吴幼雄 . 泉州宗教石刻（增订本）[M]. 北京：科学出版社，2005.

[12] 杨昌鸣，方拥 . 古城泉州 [M]. 北京：中国建筑工业出版社，2015.

[13] 泉州市文物局 . 泉州文物（国保篇）[M]. 北京：九州出版社，2021.

[14] 汪勃，吕秀家 . 泉州城考古学术研讨会论文集 [M]. 北京：科学出版社，2021.

[15] 傅晶，王敏，梁中荟，任远，王超一 . 泉州：宋元中国的世界海洋商贸中心——系列遗产整体价值及要素构成研究 [J]. 自然与文化遗产研究，2021，6.

[16] 泉州赵宋南外宗正司研究会 . 南外天源赵氏族谱 [M]. 泉州赵宋南外宗正司研究会，1994.

[17] [美] 贾志扬 . 天潢贵胄：宋代宗室史 [M]. 南京：江苏人民出版社，2010.

[18] 何兆泉 . 两宋宗室研究：以制度考察为中心 [M]. 上海：上海古籍出版社，2016.

[19] 泉州赵宋南外宗正司研究会 . 赵宋南外宗与泉州 [M]. 厦门：厦门大学出版社，2016.

[20] 泉州海外交通史博物馆 . 泉州湾宋代海船发掘与研究（修订版）[M]. 北京：海洋出版社，2017.

[21] 林瀚 . 南宋泉州南外宗正司史事考略 [J]. 福建文博 .2020，2.

[22] 黄伟 . 刺桐宋韵：南外宗赵氏与泉州 [M]. 北京：经济日报出版社，2020.

[23] 中国社会科学院考古研究所，福建博物院，泉州市海上丝绸之路申遗中心 . 泉州南外宗正司遗址 2019 年度考古发掘报告 [M]. 北京：科学出版社，2020.

[24] 汪勃，梁源 . 唐宋泉州城空间格局下的泉州南外宗正司、泉州市舶司遗址的考古发掘研究 [J]. 自然与文化遗产研究，2021，6.

[25] 中国社会科学院考古研究所，福建博物院，福建省考古研究所，泉州市海上丝绸之路申遗中心 . 泉州城遗址考古发掘报告：泉州南外宗正司遗址 2020 年 · 泉州市舶司遗址 2019 ~ 2021 年 [M]. 北京：科学出版社，2022.

[26] 泉州府文庙文物保护管理处 . 泉州府文庙碑文录 [M]. 福州：海潮摄影艺术出版社，2009.

[27] 何振良 . 略论孔庙与闽台文化交流 [J]. 泉州师范学院学报，2010，1.

[28] 方拥，杨昌鸣 . 泉州开元寺 [M]. 北京：中国建筑工业出版社，2016.

[29] 王寒枫 . 泉州东西塔 [M]. 福州：福建人民出版社，1992.

[30] 杨湘贤 . 泉州东西塔雕刻 [M]. 北京：文化艺术出版社，2007.

[31] [德] 古斯塔夫 · 埃克，[法] 保罗 · 戴密微 . 刺桐双塔 [M]. 北京：九州出版社，2018.

[32] 释元贤，释超弘 . 温陵开元寺志 瘦松集 [M]. 北京：商务印书馆，2019.

[33] 孙群 . 泉州古塔的建筑特征与文化内涵研究 [M]. 北京：九州出版社，2021.

[34] 泉州市区道教文化研究会 . 泉州道教 [M]. 厦门：鹭江出版社，1993.

[35] 方拥，杨昌鸣 . 泉州老君岩的宋代建筑构件 [J]. 华侨大学学报 (自然科学版)，1995，4.

[36] 泉州清源山风景名胜区管理委员会 . 清源山摩崖选粹 [M]. 北京：中华书局，2004.

[37] 陈达生 . 泉州伊斯兰教石刻 [M]. 福州：福建人民出版社，1984.

[38] 陈达生，王连茂 . 海上丝绸之路研究（1）. 海上丝绸之路与伊斯兰文化 [M]. 福州：福建教育出版社，1997.

[39] 陈达生 . 海上丝绸之路研究（4）. 陈达生伊斯兰教与阿拉伯碑铭研究论文集 [M]. 福州：福建教育出版社，2007.

[40] 丁毓玲，林瀚 . 涨海声中：福建与波斯、阿拉伯 [M]. 福州：福建教育出版社，2018.

[41] [法] 沙畹 . 摩尼教流行中国考 [M]. 北京：商务印书馆，1931.

[42] 林悟殊 . 古代摩尼教 [M]. 北京：商务印书馆，1983.

[43] 林悟殊 . 宋元滨海地域明教非海路输入辨 [J]. 中山大学学报 (社会科学版). 2005，03.

[44] 粘良图 . 晋江草庵研究 [M]. 厦门：厦门大学出版社，2008.

[45] 林悟殊 . 晋江摩尼教草庵发现始末考述 [J]. 福建师范大学学报 (哲学社会科学版). 2010，01.

图书在版编目（CIP）数据

美美与共：宋元泉州的多元社群：汉英对照 / 中共泉州市委宣传部编．．--福州：福建人民出版社，2024.6（2025.3重印）
（世遗之城：泉州）
ISBN 978-7-211-09042-6

Ⅰ．①美… Ⅱ．①中… Ⅲ．①社会团体—史料—泉州—宋元时期—汉、英 Ⅳ．①C232.573

中国国家版本馆 CIP 数据核字（2023）第 079030 号

美美与共——宋元泉州的多元社群
MEIMEI YUGONG——SONGYUAN QUANZHOU DE DUOYUAN SHEQUN

特约撰稿：林　瀚
翻　　译：李广伟　胡大伟　李宝虎　钟　薇　石侦霖
责任编辑：周跃进
美术编辑：陈培亮
责任校对：李雪莹
装帧设计：雅昌（上海）设计中心
出版发行：福建人民出版社　　电　　话：0591-87533169(发行部)
网　　址：http://www.fjpph.com　　电子邮箱：fjpph7211@126.com
地　　址：福州市东水路 76 号　　邮政编码：350001
经　　销：福建新华发行（集团）有限责任公司
印　　刷：雅昌文化（集团）有限公司
地　　址：深圳市南山区深云路 19 号
电　　话：0755-86083235
开　　本：787 毫米×1092 毫米　1/16
印　　张：11.75
字　　数：301 千字
版　　次：2024 年 6 月第 1 版
印　　次：2025 年 3 月第 2 次印刷
书　　号：ISBN 978-7-211-09042-6
定　　价：58.00 元

本书如有印装质量问题，影响阅读，请直接向承印厂调换。